INTERNET AND ELECTRONIC COMMERCE LAW IN THE EUROPEAN UNION

Internet and Electronic Commerce Law in the European Union

JOHN DICKIE, LLB, MA
The University of Warwick

·HART·
PUBLISHING
OXFORD – PORTLAND OREGON
1999

Hart Publishing
Oxford and Portland, Oregon

Published in North America (US and Canada) by
Hart Publishing
c/o International Specialized Book Services
5804 NE Hassalo Street
Portland, Oregon
97213-3644
USA

Distributed in the Netherlands, Belgium and Luxembourg by
Intersentia, Churchillaan 108
B2900 Schoten
Antwerpen
Belgium

Distributed in Australia and New Zealand by
Federation Press
John St
Leichhardt
NSW 2000

Hart Publishing Ltd is a specialist legal publisher based in Oxford, England.
To order further copies of this book or to request a list of other
publications please write to:

Hart Publishing Ltd, 19 Whitehouse Road, Oxford, OX1 4PA
Telephone: +44 (0)1865 434459 or Fax: +44 (0)1865 794882
e-mail: mail@hartpub.co.uk

British Library Cataloguing in Publication Data
Data Available
ISBN 1 84113–031–1 (paperback)

Typeset by Hope Services (Abingdon) Ltd.
Printed in Great Britain on acid-free paper
by Biddles Ltd, Guildford and King's Lynn.

Preface

EU Internet and electronic commerce law is novel, immature, volatile and complex. These factors have dictated my approach to writing this book. When I began, no book had been published on the subject (this is still the case as far as I am aware) and in that light, I decided to write a broad outline rather a detailed text. I hope to be able to write a second edition and am thus particularly keen to encourage readers' comments, which can be sent to <john.dickie@warwick.ac.uk> or <salsajohn@hotmail.com>.

This book is aimed at those interested in EU Internet and electronic commerce law from academic, legal, policy, and commercial perspectives. I would like to use this preface to alert interested readers to a related conference I am planning to hold at some point in 2000; registrations of interest can be sent to the e-mail addresses above.

My thanks are offered to all those who have supported me in the course of writing this book, in particular Jean Allix and his colleagues at the European Commission, Hugh Beale, Martyn Bond, Lesley Hitchens, Geraint Howells, Duncan Matthews, Mike McConville, Ursula Pachl, Abdul Paliwala, Steve Weatherill, Chris Willett, the School of Law at the University of Warwick, and the Society of Public Teachers of Law. Hart Publishing has done a tremendous job in overseeing this project from its inception. Responsibility for the content of this book is mine alone.

Thanks also to Kluwer Academic Publishers for permission to reproduce parts of J. Dickie, "Consumer Confidence and the EC Directive on Distance Contracts", 21 [1998] *Journal of Consumer Policy* 217.

This book is dedicated to Anne Dickie and May Clarke.

John Dickie
University of Warwick, summer 1999.

Contents

Abbreviations

ABA	American Bar Association
AC	Appeal Cases
ACM	Automatic Calling Machine
All ER	All England Law Reports
BEUC	Bureau Européen des Unions de Consommateurs
CD-ROM	Compact Disc – Read-Only Memory
CFSP	Common Foreign and Security Policy
CJQ	Civil Justice Quarterly
CLSR	Computer Law and Security Report
CMLR	Common Market Law Reports
CMLRev	Common Market Law Review
DTI	Department of Trade and Industry
EC	European Community
ECR	European Court Reports
ECU	European Currency Unit
EDI	Electronic Data Interchange
EFTA	European Free Trade Association
EIPR	European Intellectual Property Review
ELR	European Law Review
ERA	Europäische Rechtsakademie
EU	European Union
FTC	Federal Trade Commission
ICC	International Chamber of Commerce
IJLIT	International Journal of Law and Information Technology
JBL	Journal of Business Law
JCP	Journal of Consumer Policy
JIBL	Journal of International Banking Law
JILT	Journal of Information Law and Technology
KB	King's Bench
MLR	Modern Law Review
NCC	National Consumer Council
OECD	Organisation of Economic Cooperation and Development
OJ	Official Journal of the European Communities
OUP	Oxford University Press
TEDIS	Trade Electronic Data Interchange Systems
TRIPS	Trade-Related Aspects of Intellectual Property Rights
UNCITRAL	United Nations Commission on International Trade Law
USC	United States Code
VAT	Value-Added Tax
WCT	World Copyright Treaty
WPPT	World Performances and Phonograms Treaty
WTO	World Trade Organisation
YBEL	Yearbook of European Law

Table of Cases

European Community

United Kingdom

Table of Legislation

Table of Treaties and Conventions

1

Introduction

1.1 THE NATURE AND GROWTH OF ELECTRONIC COMMERCE

This book seeks to outline and analyse the European Community's efforts to regulate electronic commerce. Community law governs the world's largest single market, one of fifteen countries and over 370 million consumers.[1] This market is set to grow with the addition of new Member States.[2] Within the Community electronic commerce is growing at an explosive rate, fuelled by ever-improving technology and the myriad forces of globalisation. It has been suggested that in thirty years up to 30 per cent of consumer purchases will take place electronically.[3]

What is "electronic commerce"? The OECD has put it thus:

> "Electronic Commerce refers generally to all forms of commercial transactions involving both organisations and individuals, that are based upon the electronic processing and transmission of data, including text, sound and visual images. It also refers to the effects that the electronic exchange of commercial information may have on the institutions and processes that support and govern commercial activities."[4]

A typical modern transaction might be the purchase of music over the Internet, downloaded or sent on a CD-ROM via the mail. Electronic commerce has existed for many years. It has traditionally been used by closed groups under "master agreements". However, the advent of the Internet has altered the structure of the market and expanded its scope, as Table 1.1 shows.[5]

Modern electronic commerce involves all types of economic actors, including large manufacturers, small-scale retailers and consumers. New commercial functions are springing up all the time. Logistics companies store and distribute the stock of virtual shops. Brokers and searchers are used to locate particular goods and services. Catalogue aggregators provide "one-stop shops" where buyers can select different products from the cheapest shops. Buyers gain access

---

[1] Community commercial law is also generally applicable to the three additional countries that are within the European Economic Area (Iceland, Norway and Liechtenstein), and is shadowed by a number of countries who want to join the Union. The next largest market after that of the Community is that of the USA, which has 260 million consumers. The North American Free Trade Association is larger than the European Community but cannot be described as a single market.

[2] Five countries have satisfied the preliminary conditions for membership and are expected to join by 2003: Hungary, the Czech Republic, Estonia, Poland and Lithuania.

[3] "Electronic Commerce Survey", *The Economist*, 10 May 1997.

[4] OECD, *Electronic Commerce: Opportunities and Challenges for Government (The "Sacher Report")*, (Paris, OECD, 1997) at 11.

[5] Commission, *A European Initiative in Electronic Commerce* (COM(97) 157) at I(2).

Table 1.1: Traditional e-commerce compared with Internet e-commerce

Traditional e-commerce	*Internet* e-commerce
• business to business only	• business to consumers
	• business to business
	• business to public administration
	• user to user
• closed "clubs", often industry-specific	• open marketplace, unlimited partners
• closed proprietary networks	• open networks
• known and trusted partners	• known and unknown partners
• security part of network design	• security and authentication needed
• THE MARKET IS A CLUB	• THE NETWORK IS THE MARKET

to goods and services that were previously beyond their geographical or financial reach. The converse of this is also true, sellers gain access to markets which were previously beyond their reach. Individualised information provision is available free at the point of delivery, funded purely be advertising. Electronic commerce lowers entry barriers, expands existing markets and creates new markets.

1.2 LEGAL ISSUES IN ELECTRONIC COMMERCE

To gain some perspective on the types of problems which the Community has to address, listed below are four examples, taken from the Commission's *Communication on the need for strengthened international coordination in the global electronic marketplace*,[6] of electronic commerce scenarios which give rise to legal issues:

Tax: "The musical content of CDs is delivered on-line from country A to Country B; i.e. no physical goods are sent, the "music" is simply downloaded by the customers. Unlike a hard-copy, it passes from supplier to consumer without being subject to customs controls. Country B is unable to collect the VAT unless it is voluntarily declared by the resident consumer. Furthermore, a supplier in country B would be obliged to charge VAT on all sales, leaving him at a disadvantage. To put both suppliers on an equal footing, the tax regime would require modifications which might involve charging VAT on the basis of the location of the customers."

Copyright: "Country A provides for an exception to the right of communication to the public (on-line) for teaching and scientific research. Country B does not. A university in Country A includes, on the basis of the research/teaching exception, works protected by copyright in its site without the authorisation of the right holder. The site is

[6] Commission, *Globalisation and the Information Society, The Need for Strengthened International Co-ordination* (COM(98) 50), at 6–8.

accessible in Country B. The university therefore infringes rights which exist in country B and in any other country where it is accessible. The university must ensure that it has authorisation, if necessary, in all countries where the site is accessible."

Data Protection: "An individual in Country A visits the web-site of a company based in Country B. The web-site, before allowing entry, requires all users to complete an on-line questionnaire, which requests the user's personal details and other data on the user's life-style preferences. No information is given regarding the likely uses of these data. The company then sells on the information it collects to many other companies. The individual receives unsolicited e-mail messages and telephone calls from companies wishing to sell their products. The individual knows that under legislation in Country A, there is the legal right to object to the use of personal data for such purposes and that there is a national scheme to do so easily and without charge. No such legal right exists in Country B and the individual therefore has no remedy to this problem."

Contract: "A consumer in Country A desires to purchase a product from a company in Country B over the Internet. As part of the on-line offer, the consumer is supposed to accept the company's general terms and conditions, which are quite lengthy, by clicking 'OK'. The consumer does click 'OK', but did not read the terms and conditions as he would have had to stay on-line too long. When the product develops a defect, the company defends itself based on the disclaimer of liability in the on-line terms and conditions, which the consumer claims should not apply since the law of Country A requires terms and conditions to be of reasonable length and complexity."

1.3 COMMUNITY REGULATION OF ELECTRONIC COMMERCE

The Community has been involved in the regulation of electronic commerce for over a decade. The foundations of Community activity were laid in 1987 with the establishment of the TEDIS Electronic Data Interchange (EDI) programme, which had the objective of encouraging the use of EDI in trade.[7] From this has developed the range of activity which is surveyed in this book.

Whilst this book concerns itself mostly with the private law infrastructure of the Community electronic marketplace, note should also be made of the Community's progress in harmonising the technical standards which underpin that marketplace.[8] Two Directives were adopted in 1998 laying down procedures for the provision of information in the field of technical standards and of

---

[7] Council Decision introducing a communication network community programme on trade electronic data interchange systems (OJ 1987 L285/1) and following Decision (OJ 1991 L208/1). Compare American activity: ABA Model EDI Trading Agreement (1990) 45 *Business Law* 1717. The current situation is surveyed in: A. Mitrakas, *Open EDI and Law in Europe* (Deventer, Kluwer, 1997); A. Troye, "The Development of Legal Issues of EDI under the European Union TEDIS Programme" (1994) 1 *EDI Law Review* 195.

[8] An early overview of the issues is provided in European Parliament, *European Information Highways: Which Standards?* (Luxembourg, OOPEC, 1995), <www.ispo.cec.be/infosoc/promo/pubs/w18_en.html>.

rules on information society services.[9] These Directives create an obligation on Member States to ensure that the standards drawn up by their national bodies are communicated to the Commission and do not establish barriers to the smooth functioning of the internal market.[10] Extensive work has also been carried out to liberalise telecommunications infrastructures.[11] Legislation has been adopted or proposed on telecommunications competition,[12] interconnection,[13] a trans-European ISDN network[14] and universal service.[15] The Community is trying to improve the communications infrastructure through the establishment of high-speed, high-bandwidth Trans-European Networks, both terrestrial and satellite.[16] Although global Internet protocols are now well-established, there is still work for the Community to do in the field of standardisation. For example, there are currently twenty standards in Europe for stored value cards.[17] The Commission has encouraged both private and public sector initiatives to stimulate new information technologies[18] and has adopted a Memorandum of Understanding on Open Access to Electronic Commerce for European SMEs.[19]

In order to ensure the harmonious development of the diverse regulatory fields applicable to electronic commerce the Commission has identified the following principles as guides:

"1. No regulation for regulation's sake: in many cases, the free movement of electronic commerce services can be effectively achieved by mutual recognition of national rules and of appropriate self-regulatory codes. This means that companies engaged in

---

[9] 98/34/EC and 98/48/EC. These two Directives updated Council Directive 83/189/EEC laying down a procedure for the provision of information in the field of technical standards and regulations, OJ 1983 L109/8. See also: Council Recommendation 95/144 on common information technology security evaluation criteria, OJ 1995 L93/27; Commission Communication, *Standardization and the Global Information Society: The European Approach* (COM(96) 359); Commission Position Paper on the status of the voice telephony over the Internet, OJ 1997 C140/06.

[10] Article 2.

[11] See e.g. the Council Resolution on the principles and timetables for the liberalisation of telecommunications infrastructures, OJ 1994 C379/4; Directive 94/46/EC amending Directives 88/301/EEC and 90/388/EEC in particular with regard to satellite communications, OJ 1994 L268/15; Green Paper on the liberalisation of telecommunications infrastructure and cable TV networks (COM(94) 440). See further, C. Marsden, "The European Digital Convergence Paradigm: From Structural Pluralism to Behavioural Competition Law", (1997)/3 *Journal of Information Law and Technology*, <http://elj.warwick.ac.uk/jilt/commsreg/97_3mars/>.

[12] Directive 90/388 on competition in the markets for telecommunication services, OJ 1990 L192, amended most recently by Directive 96/19/EC, OJ 1996 L74/13.

[13] Directive 97/33/EC, OJ 1997 L199.

[14] Decision 1336/97 on a set of guidelines of the development of the EURO-ISDN as a trans-European network, OJ 1995 L282/16.

[15] Joint text of proposed Directive on the application of ONP to voice telephony and on universal service (96/0226 (COD) C-4 256/97).

[16] The Treaty provisions relating to Trans-European Networks are contained in Articles 129b–129d. For a list of legal measures relating to liberalisation of communications, see <http://www.ispo.cec.be/infosoc/legreg/>.

[17] COM(97) 157 at II(4).

[18] For example: the World Wide Web Consortium, a grouping of 160 companies, which is trying to ensure interoperability between payment systems, as well as issues such as data protection, content filtering and digital signatures; see <http://www.w3.org>; the Innovation Action Plan (COM(96) 589).

[19] COM(97) 157 at II(3).

cross-border business operate under the law of the country of origin ("home country control"). Only where mutual recognition does not suffice to remove obstacles in the market or to protect general interest objectives, will there be a need for Community action. Any legislative action should impose the fewest possible burdens on the market and keep pace with market developments.

2. Any regulation must be based on all Single Market freedoms: electronic commerce cuts across a wide range of cross-border activities. Whether companies engaged in electronic commerce are providing one or several goods and/or services, freedom to do so—easily and effectively—must be at the heart of future policies. Equal weight must be given to all the freedoms offered by the Single Market: the realisation of the free movement of goods, persons, services and capital together with the freedom of establishment. Only in this way can the crucial objectives of coherence, predictability and operational simplicity be achieved.

3. Any regulation must take account of business realities: in any electronic commerce operation, a trader needs to set up business, to promote its products or services and to sell, deliver and finance them. This is part of the normal process of trading—a commercial chain. In many cases, legislation will not be necessary to tackle actual or potential problems. Where it does, it must seek to facilitate operations throughout the commercial chain, for it makes no sense to remove barriers in only one part of that chain whilst leaving others untouched.

4. Any regulation must meet general interest objectives effectively and efficiently: a Single Market for electronic commerce will not develop without the effective safeguarding of recognised general interest objectives such as privacy or consumer protection and other public interests such as wide accessibility to the networks. Without such protection there is a real risk that national regulatory borders will remain in place as individual Member States seek to safeguard the legitimate concerns of their citizens."[20]

To ensure that there is a single legal system for electronic commercial activity in the Community, regulation needs to cover each step of that activity and it is instructive to break down those steps. The first step is that of establishment. Differing national regulations could inhibit the establishment of cross-border providers of goods and services, relating to professional requirements, prudential and supervisory systems, and notification or licensing requirements. The second step is that of promoting goods and services through advertising, direct marketing, self-promotions, sponsorship and public relations: what can be classified as "commercial communications". The third step in electronic commercial activity is transacting, including both consumer and business transactions, and those concluded wholly or partially at a distance. The fourth step is making payment, a field in which the principle objective of Community regulation will be ensuring compatibility between different proprietary and national systems. A fifth step may be post-transaction disagreements and Community regulation needs to ensure the existence of adequate dispute resolution systems.

---

[20] COM(97) 157 at III(2).

1.4 COMMUNITY ACTIVITY IN A GLOBAL CONTEXT

The Commission has expressed the view that the Community must move quickly if it is to make a positive contribution to the shaping of the global electronic marketplace,[21] and has stated that it aims to have a regulatory framework in place by the year 2000.[22] Whilst construction of this regulatory framework is progressing, it seems unlikely that it will be in place by 2000. In particular, the important Draft Directives on a legal framework for electronic commerce and electronic signatures, discussed in Chapters 3 and 4 below, have not yet been adopted and have no chance of being implemented by 2000.

The Community has contributed to the lowering of technical barriers to the global electronic marketplace. The Community is a signatory to the World Trade Organisation (WTO) agreement on basic telecommunication services (1997) and the ITA agreement on tariffs for information technology products. It has also signed the World Intellectual Property Organisation agreement on the protection of intellectual property,[23] and the 1993 WTO agreement on services. In those agreements the Community committed itself, together with the Member States, to the progressive liberalisation of the global electronic marketplace. The telecommunications agreement, which entered into force in January 1998, promises to be particularly significant. Sixty-nine countries signed it and all signatory states have implemented, or are in the process of implementing, the agreement through national regulatory measures.

In an attempt to co-ordinate disjointed national regulatory systems, the Commission has proposed an "International Charter for Electronic Commerce", to be agreed by, or in the course of, 1999.[24] The Charter would be non-binding and would:

> "—be a multi-lateral understanding on a method of co-ordination to remove obstacles for the global electronic marketplace,
> —recognise the work of existing international organisations,
> —promote the participation of private sector and relevant social groups,
> —contribute to more regulatory transparency".[25]

---

[21] COM(98) 50 at 2. An opinion amplified by Andersen Consulting in *eCommerce in Europe* (1998, <http://www.ac.com>). It is already possible to see the influence of national and sub-national laws at the supra-national level. For example, Germany's Federal Information and Communications Services Act 1997 (Informations- und Kommunikationsdienste Gesetz (IuKDG), English translation: <http://www.iid.de/rahmen/iukdge.html>), was a major influence on the Community's subsequent Bonner Declaration of the same year (http://www2.echo.lu/bonn/final.html). See generally, A. Boss, "Electronic Commerce and the Symbiotic Relationship Between International and Domestic Law Reform" (1998) 72 *Tulane Law Review* 1931.

[22] COM(97) 157 at III(1).

[23] See further, Commission, *Communication on the need for strengthened international co-ordination* (COM(98) 50) <www.ispo.cec.be/eif/policy/com9850en.html>, at 2.

[24] Ibid. at 11.

[25] <http://www.imsnricc.org/>. See also for an example of a national website designed to warn of "scams", <http://www.ftc.gov> (in the USA). See in the Community context, Commission, *Proposal for aCouncil Decision adopting a Community pluri-annual action plan promoting the safe use of the Internet* (COM(97) 582).

The Community also plays a global role in the supervision of marketing. In 1991 the International Marketing Supervision Network[26] was created at a Community-sponsored meeting of European consumer-law enforcement bodies in Copenhagen. The Network deals with complaints by public bodies and individual consumers, and concerns itself principally with the Internet. The Commission represents the Community interest within the Network, which now meets under the auspices of the Organisation for Economic Cooperation and Development and includes many countries from outside the Community.

The International Marketing Supervision Network is a good jumping-off point for analysis of the problems thrown up by the international nature of the electronic marketplace. The Network's coverage is incomplete and there are wide differences in approach between participating countries. For example, Italy has not joined the network because it does not have a public body responsible for the enforcement of consumer law,[27] Germany is represented by a nongovernmental body which has no executive power, and the USA has had problems in becoming a full contributing member because of a statutory limitation on the ability of the Federal Trade Commission (FTC) to provide information to foreign authorities.[28]

[27] COM(97) 582 at 17.
[28] Under the Federal Trade Commission Act, s. 21. This provision was originally enacted to protect the confidentiality of ongoing FTC investigations (R. Starek, "Consumer Protection in the Age of Borderless Markets and the Information Revolution", <www.ftc.gov/speeches/starek/ausp. htm>).

2

Financial Services and Taxation

This chapter deals first with financial services and secondly with taxation. Electronic commerce involves financial services in two ways. First, services such as insurance policies and pensions can be sold electronically. Secondly, payment in electronic commerce will often involve a financial service, such as credit or electronic money. In relation to the former, the Commission in 1998 adopted a Draft Directive on the distance marketing of financial services. In relation to the latter, a variety of Community instruments are of relevance, relating to consumer credit, cross-border credit transfers, electronic payment instruments and electronic money.

2.1 DRAFT DIRECTIVE ON THE DISTANCE MARKETING OF FINANCIAL SERVICES

The distance marketing of financial services throws up a variety of problems for Community law including in particular the protection of consumers from rogue suppliers and the minimisation of conflicts between Member States' laws. The Commission has put forward a framework to deal with these problems in its Draft Directive on the distance marketing of financial services.[1] These problems are also to be found in the distance marketing of other goods and services, which the Community dealt with in the 1997 Directive on distance contracts.[2] At the behest of the Council, the Directive on distance contracts excluded financial services from its scope, for two reasons. First, it was considered necessary to examine the extent of protection offered by existing directives on financial services before fresh legislation was introduced.[3] Secondly, it was considered that the specific nature of financial services necessitated special treatment.[4] The "specific nature" of financial services was not elaborated on and it is not clear what was meant by this. If a consumer is to be protected when he buys a car, a holiday, or

---

[1] Commission, *Proposal for a Directive of the European Parliament and Council concerning the distance marketing of consumer financial services and modifying Directives 90/619/EEC (life assurance), 97/7/EC (distance contracts) and 98/27/EC (injunctions)*, (COM(1998) 468), henceforth "*Proposal for a Directive*".

[2] Directive 97/7/EC, discussed in Chapter 9 below.

[3] See *Proposal for a Directive*, n. 1 above at 4. It should be said that the lobbying power of the financial services industry may have played a part in their exclusion from the Directive on distance contracts. See also the special provision made for insurance contracts in the Directive 13/93/EEC on unfair terms in consumer contracts, discussed in Chapter 8 below.

[4] *Proposal for a Directive*, n. 1 above, at 4.

a computer program at a distance, there seems little reason why he should not also be protected when he buys an insurance policy or a pension at a distance.

Further to the Council's insistence on the need for special treatment of financial services, the Commission compared existing Directives on financial services with the Directive on distance contracts and found that, in contrast with the Directive on distance contracts, existing financial services Directives did not provide for the following:

> "—the written confirmation (on paper or in another durable medium) of the contract (with the exception of consumer credit and life assurance);
> —the right of withdrawal (with the exception of life assurance);
> —the ban on inertia selling;
> —rules governing unsolicited communications;
> —rules that apply when the service is not available;
> —rules designed to establish basic principles governing the resolution of disputes."[5]

In response to these gaps, and calls for legislation by the European Parliament[6] and the European Council,[7] the Commission in 1998 produced its Draft Directive.[8] Although the Commission had in 1997 called on industry and consumers to agree voluntary improvements in the provision of information,[9] this was evidently not forthcoming, and the rapid growth in the distance selling of financial services seems to have pushed the Commission to action.[10]

The current lacuna of regulation relating to the distance marketing of financial services poses the danger that consumers will be vulnerable to fraudulent suppliers of financial services. The principle of mutual recognition provides that goods and services legitimately supplied in one Member State can only be regulated by another Member State if due cause can be shown.[11] This is the case even if the regulating Member State in question is seeking to apply to foreign suppliers the rules which it applies internally.[12] This creates danger for consumers who will typically not be in a good position to assess the nature of a foreign

---

[5] *Proposal for a Directive*, n. 1 above, at 4. The only overlaps were in disjointed provision for pre- and post-contract information.

[6] Parliament Resolution of 17 February 1997 on the Commission Green Paper, "Financial services—meeting consumers' expectations" (A4–0048/97, PE 220.154/fin). In the same document the Parliament called for the introduction of a Community legal framework for all financial services.

[7] See Amsterdam European Council Action Plan for the Single Market (SCE(97) 1), 4 June 1997.

[8] *Proposal for a Directive*, n. 1 above.

[9] COM(97) 309 final at 7, giving industry and consumers 18 months (until mid-1999) to make sufficient progress.

[10] The Commission has noted that some markets, such as those for car insurance and investment products, already have a significant cross-border element: Commission Communication, *Financial Services: Enhancing Consumer Confidence* (COM(97)309) at 5.

[11] Under Articles 28 and 49 of the EC Treaty. See especially *Rewe-Zentral AG v Bundesmonopolverwaltung für Branntwein* ("*Cassis de Dijon*") Case 120/78 [1979] ECR 649.

[12] "Reverse discrimination" is not prohibited by EC law. See *R v Saunders* Case 175/78 [1979] ECR 1129; W. Pickup, "Reverse Discrimination and Freedom of Movement of Workers" (1986) 23 *CMLRev* 135. The Court has in many cases given primacy to enhancing market integration rather than to protecting consumers, see e.g., *Commission v Germany* ("*German Sparkling Wine*") Case 179/85 [1986] ECR 3879.

financial service or the standing of its provider, as they do not typically possess expert knowledge of financial services.[13] These problems are exacerbated by language differences, geographical distance, and the complexity and expense of many financial services. Further, the high value of financial services make them attractive to fraudulent suppliers.

The aim of the Draft Directive is to harmonise Member States' rules on the distance marketing of financial services.[14] Only the method of selling is within the scope of the Draft Directive; it does not seek to regulate the content of such services. "Financial service" is defined by reference to relevant Community instruments,[15] whilst "consumer" is defined as "any natural person resident in the territory of the European Community who, in contracts covered by this Directive, is acting for purposes which are outside his trade, business, or profession".[16]

The centrepiece of the Draft Directive is the granting to consumers of a "reflection period" prior to the conclusion of any contract.[17] Suppliers must communicate all the terms and conditions of any proposed contract to the consumer in writing or another durable medium.[18] These terms must be valid for a minimum of fourteen days (except in the case of services of fluctuating price such as foreign exchange[19]). The reflection period ensures that consumers have time to make a reasoned judgement on an offer, and to compare other offers if they wish. Where the consumer does not wait until the end of the reflection period to conclude the contract, he obtains a "cooling-off period" of fourteen days.[20] If he concludes the contract after the reflection period, he receives no cooling-off period. The consumer has to pay a certain amount to the supplier if he exercises his right to withdraw in certain specific circumstances, for example where the supplier has expended money valuing a property pursuant to a loan

---

[13] As an example of the inability of consumers to understand financial services, see Office of Fair Trading, *Consumers' appreciation of "Annual Percentage Rates"* (London, OFT, 1994).

[14] Article 1.

[15] "Any service provided by credit institutions, insurance companies or investment firms coming within the scope of the Second Council Directive 89/646/EEC of 15 December 1989 on the co-ordination of laws, regulations and administrative provisions relating to the taking up and pursuit of the business of credit institutions and amending Directive 77/780/EEC, Council Directive 93/22/EEC of 10 May 1993 on investment services in the securities field, Council Directive 73/239/EEC of 24 July 1973 on the co-ordination of laws, regulations and administrative provisions relating to the taking-up and pursuit of the business of direct insurance other than life assurance, and Council Directive 79/267/EEC of 5 March 1979 on the co-ordination of laws, regulations and administrative provisions relating to the taking up and pursuit of the business of direct life assurance, and an indicative list of which is provided in the Annex" (Article 2(b)).

[16] Article 2(d).

[17] Article 3. Also to be found in Directive 94/47/EC on Timeshare Contracts.

[18] For example e-mail or a CD-ROM: Article 2(f).

[19] In the case of such services, the terms must still be sent to the consumer, but the price is given on an indicative basis only, it is fixed, with the express consent of the consumer, at the time the contract is concluded (Article 3(4)).

[20] Article 4. The cooling-off period is extended to 30 days for mortgage loans, life assurance and personal pensions. There is no cooling-off period in cases of non-life insurance policies of less than one month's duration, nor in sales of financial products whose price depends on market fluctuations outside the supplier's control (Article 4(1)).

contract, or where the supplier has insured the consumer for a certain number of days before withdrawal.[21]

The Draft Directive places stress on the provision of information to the consumer, requiring suppliers to inform consumers in a clear and comprehensible manner of the existence and scope of the right of reflection and right of withdrawal.[22] Further, amendment is made to two Directives on consumer credit and life assurance which contain certain requirements of writing on a paper medium. The Draft Directive provides that writing on any durable medium such as floppy disk, CD-ROM or e-mail, will satisfy these requirements.[23]

Whilst the consumer has a reflection period, this does not automatically mean that the financial service will be available at the time requested. For example, a consumer may request that a supplier purchase a certain number of shares when a company increases its capital, and this number of shares may be unavailable to the supplier on the day of issue.[24] In such cases, the supplier must inform the consumer, and reimburse any sums paid, without undue delay.[25]

The unsolicited supply of financial services is prohibited and the use of unsolicited communications is restricted in two ways: first, the use of automated calling systems and faxes is subject to the consumer's prior consent; secondly, with regard to other media, Member States are free to choose between a system of prior consent or a "Robinson list" system whereby consumers can register themselves as unwilling to receive unsolicited communications.[26]

The Draft Directive provides that consumers may not waive the rights therein conferred on them,[27] and further that:

> "consumers may not be deprived of the protection granted by this Directive when the law governing the contract is that of a country that does not belong to the European Community, when the consumer is resident on the territory of a Member State of the European Community and when the contract has a close link with the Community" (Article 11(3)).

The meaning of "close link" is unclear. The same wording is used in the Directive on distance contracts and analysis of this phrase is made in Chapter 9 below.

The Draft Directive provides that effective complaints and redress procedures must be put in place for the settlement of disputes between consumers and suppliers.[28] These procedures must enable public bodies, consumer organisations and professional organisations to take relevant enforcement action before the courts or competent administrative bodies. This networking of enforcement

---

[21] Article 5.
[22] Article 6.
[23] Articles 2(f) and 7.
[24] See *Proposal for a Directive*, n. 1 above, at 14.
[25] Article 8.
[26] Articles 9, 10(1) and 10(2) respectively. See also the similar provisions within the Directive on distance contracts, Chapter 9 below.
[27] Article 11(1).
[28] Article 12(1).

responsibility is likely to prove effective as having three types of potential enforcers greatly diminishes the risk of inadequate enforcement due to any one body being unable or unwilling to take action. Further, the Draft Directive provides that Member States shall encourage the public or private bodies responsible for dispute settlement to co-operate in settling cross-border disputes. Although this provision is to be welcomed in that it acknowledges the existence of barriers to cross-border dispute settlement, it does not lay down any firm rules and it is unclear what impact it might have.

2.2 DRAFT DIRECTIVES ON ELECTRONIC MONEY INSTITUTIONS

Electronic money is one of the fastest growing off-shoots of electronic commerce. Whilst credit and debit cards are currently the most widely-used media for making electronic payment,[29] and their payment settlement systems are well-established and involve global companies with extensive assets and substantial experience, use of electronic money is growing rapidly. References to electronic money ("e-money") will be most relevant to electronic cash, as whilst electronic cheques do exist they are almost identical to traditional electronic funds transfer.[30] Electronic cash works by transferring an electronic token from the buyer to the seller, which may or may not then be presented by the seller to the bank for payment.[31] This differs from electronic funds transfer, which involves the transferral of bank debt from customer to retailer. The attractiveness of electronic cash over card payment lies particularly in the fact that it does away with the risk that card details will fall into the wrong hands if transmitted over open networks.[32]

Electronic cash throws up novel legal problems. It is currently issued by private parties who do not have the financial stability of the national banks which underwrite "hard" cash. This public underwriting came about many years ago as a solution to the problems caused by the instability of private banks, which is in effect what issuers of e-cash are. The legal basis of e-cash is a contractual one.

---

[29] The number of payments by card per inhabitant has increased from 7 in 1990 to 14 in 1995 (including credit, debit and "stored value" cards). Their share of all payment transactions grew from 9% to 13.5% over the same period: Communication from the Commission, *Boosting Customers' Confidence in Electronic Means of Payment in the Single Market* (COM(97) 353 final). See also Communication from the Commission, *A European Initiative on Electronic Commerce* (COM(97) 157).

[30] As an example of a highly public "e-cheque": in June 1998 the US Treasury sent a $32,000 e-cheque to a supplier, the cheque was electronically endorsed by the supplier and electronically deposited at the Bank of Boston, see <http://www.bos.frb.org/finance/empayments/indexf.htm>.

[31] For some examples of systems which are currently running, see <www.emoney.ru>; <www.mondex.com>; <www.digicash.com>; <www.visa.com/cgi-bin/vee/nt/epay/main.html>.

[32] "Packet sniffer" programs can search messages on open networks for strings of numbers similar to those on payment cards. This is the reason why there is more concern over the security of computer networks than there is over giving numbers out over the telephone network, which cannot be "searched" in the same way.

There is a standing unilateral offer on behalf of the banks to convert into traditional cash the electronic cash which they originated.[33]

In 1998 the Commission adopted two Draft Directives on the regulation of electronic money institutions.[34] This was a response to a call from the European Council at Cardiff.[35] The aims of the Draft Directives are to create both legal certainty and a "single passport" for electronic money institutions throughout the Community.[36] The Draft Directives are particularly significant for electronic commerce as they foreshadow the ability of buyers to make payments smaller than would otherwise be possible, including those of less than one euro cent or one US cent. The feasibility of such payments will be particularly important in the development of the Web as a commercial information directory. Community activity in this area is blazing a trail which may direct developments on the wider international stage.[37]

The Draft Directives identify electronic money as value on a card or in computer memory which is a digital form of cash in as much as it does not require authorisation from any third party. In this way it differs from debit cards which require a bank account, and credit cards which require the existence of a contract with a creditor. Also, electronic money can be used anonymously. The first of the two Draft Directives, the Draft Directive on electronic money institutions, lays down specific requirements for institutions wishing to issue electronic money, which it defines as:

> "monetary value which is;
>   (i) stored electronically on an electronic device such as a chip card or a computer memory;
> (ii) accepted as a means of payment by undertakings other than the issuing institution;
> (iii) generated in order to be put at the disposal of users to serve as an electronic surrogate for coins and banknotes; and
> (iv) generated for the purpose of effecting electronic transfers of limited value payments" (Article 1(3)1.2.(b)).

Thus, network money as well as cards carrying cash, such as the Proton card in Belgium, are covered by the Draft Directive, whilst single-use cards such as telephone cards are not. Only cash which is usable in three-way relationships is covered, so for example, if an Internet bookstore issues electronic vouchers

---

[33] See further, L. Davies and C. Reed, *Digital Cash—the legal implications* (London, Centre for Commercial Law Studies Queen Mary and Westfield College, 1995).

[34] Commission, *Proposal for European Parliament and Council Directives on the taking up, the pursuit and the prudential supervision of the business of electronic money institutions* (COM(98) 727).

[35] Ibid. at 1.

[36] Ibid. at 1.

[37] There is currently little regulation of e-money anywhere in the world. Japan is at the stage of conducting pilot schemes and the US Task Force on Electronic Payments, in May 1998 decided that government regulation would make electronic money unnecessarily expensive and prejudice innovation and competition (ibid. at 3).

which can only be spent in that bookstore, the bookstore is not an e-money institution within the meaning of the Draft Directive.

The Draft Directive goes on to prescribe which of the Community's banking regulations are to apply to e-money institutions.[38] Institutions which satisfy the relevant conditions are to benefit from the "European Passport" of the Second Banking Directive, entitling them to establish freely and provide services throughout the Community.[39]

Although e-money institutions are exempted from some of the Community's banking regulations, the Draft Directive sets out minimum requirements. First, institutions must have an initial capital of no less than ECU 500,000 and not allow their own funds to drop below that amount.[40] Secondly, institutions are required to invest mostly in low-risk instruments.[41] Thirdly, e-money institutions must have their operations verified by competent public authorities at least every six months.[42]

The second Draft Directive simply amends the definition of "credit institution" within the meaning of the First Banking Co-ordination Directive[43] so as to bring electronic money institutions within the scope of that Directive and thus the Community's banking regulation regime generally. In this way enterprises will be able to issue electronic money valid throughout the Community, whilst at the same time being subject to possible reserve requirements imposed by the European Central Bank.

2.3 ELECTRONIC PAYMENT SYSTEMS

The Community has for many years played a role in regulating traditional forms of electronic payment. In 1987 the Commission issued a Recommendation on a European Code of Conduct relating to electronic payment.[44] This was followed in 1988 by a Recommendation on payment systems covering both electronic and non-electronic systems.[45]

---

[38] Article 2. The relevant banking regulations are the First and Second Banking Directives (77/780/EEC, 89/646/EEC).

[39] Per *Proposal*, n. 34 above, at 10.

[40] Article 3(1). Ongoing own funds must reflect the size of their operation.

[41] Article 4.

[42] Article 5.

[43] Directive 77/780/EEC on the co-ordination of laws, regulations and administrative provisions relating to the taking up and pursuit of the business of credit institutions, OJ 1977 L322/30.

[44] Recommendation 87/598/EEC of 8 December 1987 on a European Code of Conduct relating to electronic payment (relations between financial institutions, traders and service establishments, and consumers), OJ 1987 L365/72. See also the European Credit Sector Associations' Code of Practice, *Transnational Data Report* (June/July 1990) at 9.

[45] Commission Recommendation 88/590/EEC concerning payment systems, and in particular the relationship between card holder and card issuer, OJ 1988 L317/55. See further X. Thunis, "The Second European Recommendation Concerning Payment Systems: New Obligations for Card Issuers?" (1992) 3 *JIBL* 101.

The 1988 Recommendation provides that payment devices must be supplied with a "full and fair" written contract.[46] The contract must be in the language or languages which are ordinarily used for such or similar purposes in the regions where the contract terms are offered.[47] Thus, a French device-issuer offering devices in Italy must offer a contract in Italian. There is no liability for the use of a payment device after notification of its loss, and liability prior to notification is limited to 150 ECU.[48] These restrictions apply where the device-holder has not been fraudulent or grossly negligent.[49] It is not clear what amounts to "gross negligence" in the context of electronic commerce. For example, would it be grossly negligent for a device-holder to give his payment device details to a website which gave no indication that it would accept such a device? Or for a device-holder to send details of a payment device via unencrypted e-mail or to store device details on a computer periodically attached to an external network? This latter question is particularly pertinent with regard to electronic cash. In view of the consumerist nature of the Recommendation,[50] it is likely that the negligence requirement will be interpreted generously from the point of view of a consumer device-holder. In any disputed electronic funds transfer, the Recommendation provides that the burden of proving that the transfer took place should lie with the device-issuer.[51]

The link between the development of electronic commerce and the need for a new framework for payment instruments was highlighted in 1997 by the Commission in its Communication, *A European Initiative in Electronic Commerce*.[52] The Commission stated in particular that a new Recommendation was necessary to simplify the introduction of the euro and this was subsequently forthcoming—the Recommendation on Electronic Payment Instruments 1997.[53]

The Recommendation is directed principally at innovative payment methods, including telebanking, new forms of bank cards, and electronic money products such as that stored on cards or computer memories. It maintains the liability limitation of the 1988 Recommendation, namely 150 ECU, except in cases of extreme negligence or fraud on the part of the holder where no such limit will apply.[54] It also provides that the issuer is liable for the non-execution or defec-

---

[46] Annex 3.1.

[47] Annex 3.2.

[48] Annex 8.3.

[49] It has been proposed that this provision be amended to reduce the burden on the device-holder, see G. Howells and T. Wilhelmsson, *EC Consumer Law* (Aldershot, Dartmouth, 1997) at 217.

[50] See Recital 2 in particular.

[51] Recital 11.

[52] COM(97) 157 at 6.

[53] Commission Recommendation concerning transactions by electronic payment instruments and in particular the relationship between issuer and holder, annexed to Commission Communication, *Boosting Customers' Confidence in Electronic Means of Payment* (COM(97) 353). Note should also be made of the Amsterdam European Council's Action Plan against Organised Crime, which urged Member States to ensure that their laws appropriately sanctioned abuse of electronic payment systems, and Parliament Resolution at OJ 1997 C371.

[54] Article 6. Compare the position in the USA, where the Electronic Funds Transfer Act 1978 (15 USC §1693) limits the consumer's liability for unauthorised transactions to $50 (Regulation G),

tive execution of the holder's transactions and for transactions not authorised by the holder. Member States are "invited to ensure" that there are adequate and effective means in place for the settlement of disputes between a holder and an issuer.[55]

Its core requirements are transparency, fair allocation of the parties' liabilities and adequate redress procedures. If a satisfactory level of compliance is not reached, the Commission has indicated that it will propose a Directive in order to force issuers to comply.[56] It seems likely that a Draft Directive will eventually be forthcoming in view of the fact that compliance with the 1987 Recommendation was poor[57] and there seems no reason why compliance with the 1997 Recommendation should be any better.

2.4 PAYING ACROSS BORDERS WITHIN THE COMMUNITY

Payment within the Community electronic marketplace will often involve a cross-border credit transfer. Such transfers can give rise to a number of problems, as the Commission found in a study it carried out in the area.[58] In this study the Commission found that unauthorised double charging occurred in 36 per cent of cases and 15 per cent of transfers took longer than six working days.[59] In 1997 the Community responded to these problems by adopting the Directive on cross border credit transfers,[60] which is due to be transposed into national law by August 1999.[61] The principal provision of the Directive is that credit transfers involving 50,000 ECU or less between Member States must respect the following requirements:

(1)   transfers must be credited to the beneficiary's account within six working days (unless the originator and his bank specifically agree a different time-scale);

(2)   interest is paid by the originator's bank if the transfer takes longer than six working days or the agreed delay;

except where: (1) the consumer fails to report the loss or theft of the card within two days, (2) the consumer fails to report apparently unauthorised transactions within 60 days of receiving a bank statement (Regulation E).

[55] Article 10.

[56] Commission Communication, *Boosting Customers' Confidence in Electronic Means of Payment in the Single Market* (COM(97) 353) final at 5.

[57] Knobbout-Bethlem, *A Survey of Implementation of the EC Recommendation Concerning Payment Systems* (Consumentenbond and BEUC, 1990); P. Mitchell and R. Thomas, *Payment card terms and conditions* (Edinburgh, International Consumer Policy Bureau, 1994).

[58] Commission, *Proposal for a Directive on Cross-border Credit Transfers* (COM(94) 436) at 4–6.

[59] Ibid. at 5. Further, the cost of transferring 100 ECU averaged 25 ECU. Written information on money transfers was not available at 46% of the bank branches. Where written information was available, it complied with banking industry guidelines in only 14% of cases.

[60] Directive 97/5/EC, OJ 1997 L43/25.

[61] Article 11(1).

(3)   there should be no double-charging, all charges must be paid by the originator to his bank, in which case the beneficiary's bank cannot deduct
charges from the money transferred (unless the originator has specifically
indicated that charges should be shared with the beneficiary);

(4)   if double-charging does occur, the onus will be on the originator's bank to
reimburse the beneficiary, or alternatively the originator, any sum wrongly
deducted (or in the case of unauthorised charging by beneficiary banks, the
latter will have to reimburse, free of charge, the excess fees to the beneficiary);

(5)   "lost" transfers that fail to reach the beneficiary's bank must be reimbursed
in full to the originator by the originator's bank up to a ceiling of ECU
12,500. The originator's bank must reimburse all charges and fees associated with the lost transfer and pay interest. Reimbursement will have to be
carried out within fourteen days of the customer's request, which can be
lodged after the deadline for completion of the transfer.

2.5 CONNECTED LENDER LIABILITY

A further aspect of Community financial services law which is relevant to electronic commerce is the provision made for connected lender liability in Article
11(2) of the Consumer Credit Directive.[62] This provides that when a consumer
buys goods or services on credit, the creditor will generally be jointly liable with
the supplier if the goods or services are not correctly supplied. The rationale
behind connected lender liability is that the connected lender can legitimately be
expected to underwrite the supplier. The lender will typically check the integrity
of traders before authorising them to take payment, and this enables consumers
to have some guarantee when selecting a supplier. Further, creditors are usually
in a better position to take action against defaulting suppliers than consumers.
These considerations are of importance in the borderless and intangible electronic marketplace.

The Directive provides for connected lender liability in cases where the individual transaction is for an amount between 200 and 20,000 ECU.[63] Liability
arises when "the grantor of credit and the supplier of goods or services have a
pre-existing arrangement whereunder credit is made available exclusively by
that grantor of credit to customers of that supplier for the acquisition of goods
or services".[64] Whilst the requirements of "pre-existing arrangement" and
"exclusivity" create doubt as to whether the provision applies to credit cards, it

---

[62] Council Directive 87/102/EEC for the approximation of the laws, regulations and administrative provisions of the Member States concerning consumer credit, OJ 1987 L42/48, amended by
Council Directive 90/88/EEC, OJ 1990 L61/14.

[63] Articles 11(3) and 2(1)(f). Thus, the purchase in one transaction of four software programs
worth 50 ECUs each would satisfy the requirements for connected lender liability.

[64] Article 11(2)(b).

is likely sufficient that the pre-existing agreement only exist with a sister company of the credit card company (e.g. VISA Italia, as opposed to VISA France). Further, "exclusivity" can be read as meaning applicable to the agreement in question rather than as meaning exclusively of other creditors. The creditor is not liable until the consumer has pursued his remedies against the supplier.[65] It is unclear whether or not this requires consumers to initiate legal action. In view of the consumer-protection rationale of the Directive it is likely that "pursuing his remedies" entails merely the first stage of the pursuit, i.e. a demand from the consumer. It is unlikely that the Directive requires consumers to go to court. The time and expense involved in this would intimidate many consumers to the extent of negating the value of connected lender liability.

2.6 TAX LAW

The borderless nature of the electronic marketplace creates problems for the law of indirect taxation. Within the Community, the relevant tax is Value Added Tax (VAT),[66] and the primary legislative instrument is Council Directive 77/388 generally referred to as the "Sixth Directive" (OJ 1977 L145). The area is currently under review by the Commission.[67] The Directive is not a measure of absolute harmonisation. It gives Member States autonomy in relation to certain areas, in particular the level of the standard rate of VAT.[68]

Certain supplies are exempt from VAT, for example insurance, education, banking and medical services.[69] The rules relating to these exemptions are similar throughout the Community. In respect of other supplies Member States are free to apply a zero[70] or reduced rate[71] and there are wide variations as to which supplies benefit from these rates.[72]

---

[65] Article 11(2)(e). Contrast the UK Consumer Credit Act 1975, s. 75, which establishes joint and several liability.

[66] VAT is a consumption tax. It should be distinguished from sales tax which only applies to retail sales; VAT is payable at all stages of production (it can often be claimed back by businesses). The person with legal responsibility for paying the tax is the supplier of the goods or services.

[67] Commission Communication, *Electronic Commerce and Indirect Taxation* (COM(98) 374).

[68] This can be anything up to 15%.

[69] Sixth Directive, Article 13. Education and medical services are exempt for obvious reasons, the exclusion of insurance and banking services is a tribute to the lobbying power of those sectors. See also the Directive on distance contracts, discussed in Chapter 9, from which the entire financial services sector managed to gain exemption.

[70] The difference between exempt and zero-rated goods and services relates to the ability of businesses to claim back tax paid producing the good or service.

[71] Although reduced rates should normally be no less than 5%: Sixth Directive, Article 12(3)(a).

[72] For example, while the United Kingdom zero-rates books, newspapers, children's clothes, food, and public transport, this selection of goods and services is not the same in any other Member State.

2.6.1 Goods or services?

It is necessary in relation to the taxation of electronic commerce to define whether a supply is of goods or services:

> " 'Supply of goods' shall mean the transfer of the right to dispose of tangible property as owner" (Article 5).

Sales of information or audio-visual services are not sales of tangible property and therefore cannot be supplies of goods under the Sixth Directive, which goes on to provide that where a supply is not of goods, it is of services.[73] The following electronic commerce services are thus classified as supplies of services for the purposes of VAT law:

(a)   a CD-ROM to be downloaded to the customer's CD-ROM burner;
(b)   movie transmission or "virtual video hire";
(c)   provision of advertising on a website;
(d)   software downloaded to the customer's hard disk;[74]
(e)   provision of dial-up Internet access and e-mail;
(f)   pay-per-use databases.

The result of this is as follows: where images, software, music or other data is supplied via a tangible medium it is a supply of goods within the meaning of Article 5 of the Sixth Directive and thus subject to VAT; where such data is sold via electronic communication, it is a supply of services and thus exempt from VAT. It is therefore cheaper for a consumer to buy music and software via electronic communication and this is likely to spur rapid growth of such deliveries as the necessary technology spreads.[75]

2.6.2 Import and export

Goods exported from the Community are zero-rated.[76] Community suppliers are thus attractive to the external buyer whose country does not tax imports (there are few!).[77] Within the Community, supplies of goods are taxable in the

---

[73] Article 6(1). This is provided that it is not supplied for free.

[74] Although there are a small number of differences in the treatment of software between Member States, see further Broderson, "International Tax Issues in Cyberspace: Taxation of Cross-border Electronic Commerce" (1997) 25 *Intertax* 133. The Commission has set up a Taxation Policy Group to discuss ways of achieving complete harmonisation, see *A European Initiative in Electronic Commerce* (COM(97) 157 final) at paragraph 59.

[75] This may result in supplies of data on physical media being reclassified as supplies of services, which would seem logical as the value of such lies in the data rather than the media. Evidence from the USA, which has extensive experience of differences in sales taxes between states, suggests that differentials over 5% can have substantial effect: S. Eden, "The Taxation of Electronic Commerce", in L. Edwards and C. Waelde, *Law and the Internet* (Oxford, Hart Publishing, 1997) at 154.

[76] Sixth Directive, Article 15.

[77] Most trading entities, including the Community, do tax imports.

customer's state, rather than the supplier's. Thus, if a United Kingdom trader buys goods from a German supplier, the VAT is paid to the United Kingdom authorities by the United Kingdom trader. However, there are supplier thresholds which trigger a requirement on the supplier to register for VAT in the "customer" state.[78]

Goods imported into the Community are taxable at the point of entry. Typically, customs authorities are empowered to demand VAT on mail-order goods imported from outside the Community before releasing them for delivery.[79] However, in the case of small-scale purchases, the state may not bother to levy it.[80] Services supplied from outside the Community to businesses registered for VAT are treated in the same way as imported goods. Services supplied to unregistered entities (i.e. small businesses and consumers) are VAT-free.

---

[78] In the United Kingdom this is £70,000: VAT Act 1994, Sch. 2(1).
[79] For example in the United Kingdom under the Postal Packets (Customs and Excise Regulations) 1986, SI 1986/20.
[80] This is certainly the author's experience of importing CD-ROMs for personal use into the United Kingdom from the USA.

3

Draft Directive on Electronic Commerce

As this book shows, electronic commerce draws together disparate strands of law, including those relating to commercial communications, contracts, liability, licensing and enforcement. In 1998 the Commission began an attempt to unify these strands by adopting a Draft Directive on electronic commerce.[1] This followed from the Commission's 1997 Communication on electronic commerce, which set an objective of creating a coherent Community legal framework by the year 2000,[2] an objective which received the strong support of the Parliament.[3] The Draft Directive aims to facilitate the free movement of information society services between the Member States through the country-of-origin principle of regulation.[4] Thus, Article 3(2) provides "Member States may not, for reasons falling within this Directive's co-ordinated field, restrict the freedom to provide Information Society services from another Member State". The Draft Directive's "co-ordinated field" would appear to be narrower than might be thought at first sight, as it only provides harmonised rules in relation to the place where the service provider is established, the transparency of commercial communications, the formation of electronic contracts and the liability of intermediaries. It is not clear how the principle of country of origin fits with this narrow co-ordinated field.[5]

The Commission describes the Draft Directive as adopting a "light, enabling, and flexible approach",[6] in approximating:

> "national regulations applicable to information society services; this concerns the internal market principle, the establishment of service providers, commercial communications, electronic contracts, the liability of intermediaries, codes of conduct, out of court dispute settlement systems, court actions and administrative co-operation between Member States".[7]

These areas will now be discussed in turn.

---

[1] Commission, *Proposal for a European Parliament and Council Directive on certain legal aspects of electronic commerce in the internal market* (COM(98) 586) OJ 1999 C30/4. <http://www.ispo.cec.be/ ecommerce/legal.htm> ("the Draft Directive"), reproduced in Appendix 2. The Parliament adopted a generally favourable report on 6 May 1999 (A4.0248/99).

[2] *A European Initiative in Electronic Commerce* (COM(97) 157 final) at 3. The Draft Directive provides for an implementation period of just one year (Article 25).

[3] Resolution A4–0173/98, point 14. See also ECOSOC's opinion, at OJ 1998 C19/72.

[4] Articles 1 and 3.

[5] See further, Bureau Européen des Unions de Consommateurs Position Paper on the proposal for a directive on certain legal aspects of e-commerce (Brussels, BEUC/044/99) at 3.

[6] Draft Directive at 3.

[7] Article 1(2).

The Draft Directive provides that access to the activity of "information society service provider"[8] may not be made subject to prior authorisation.[9] Thus it grants to all individuals and companies a concrete right to establish a website in particular. In line with the principle of transparency, all information service providers must make easily accessible[10] to recipients and competent authorities the following information (Article 5):

"(a) the name of the service provider;

 (b) the address at which the service provider is established;

 (c) the co-ordinates of the service provider including his electronic-mail address which allow for him to be contacted rapidly and communicated with in a direct and effective manner;

 (d) where the service provider is registered in a trade register, the trade register in which the service provider is entered and any registration number in that register;

 (e) where the activity is subject to an authorisation scheme, the activities covered by the authorisation granted to the service provider and the coordinates of the authority providing this authorisation;

 (f) as concerns the regulated professions:
      any professional body or similar institution with which the service provider is registered;
      the professional title granted in the Member State of establishment, the applicable professional rules in the Member State of establishment and the Member States in which the information society services are regularly provided;

 (g) in the case where the service provider undertakes an activity that is subject to VAT, the VAT number he is registered under with his fiscal administration".

Article 5 is concerned with minimising the dangers presented by the transient nature of information society services. In particular, it requires that providers give a geographical address.[11] Article 5 is similar to the information requirements of the Directive on distance contracts.[12] However, unlike the Directive on distance contracts, the information requirements of the Draft Directive apply whether there is a contract or not.[13] Article 5(2) of the Draft Directive provides

---

[8] A natural or legal person who provides services for remuneration, at a distance, by electronic means and at the individual request of a recipient of services (Articles 2(a) and (b) in summary).

[9] Article 4. This is without prejudice to the regulatory provisions of Directive 97/13/EC on a common framework for general authorisations and individual licences in the field of telecommunications services.

[10] The Draft Directive (at 20) states that an icon with a hypertext link to the information would be sufficient to meet this requirement.

[11] Article 5(b). The reference to "address" must relate to the service provider's geographical address, as Article 5(c) deals with its "co-ordinates", including its e-mail address.

[12] Articles 4 and 5, discussed in Chapter 9 below.

[13] The relevant provisions of the Directive on distance contracts applies only where there is a contractual or proto-contractual relationship.

that prices must be given accurately and unequivocally, and it is indicated that a price in euros would meet this requirement.[14]

3.2 COMMERCIAL COMMUNICATIONS

The Draft Directive demonstrates that there is a considerable need for harmonisation in the area of commercial communications, including advertising, marketing and sponsorship.[15] These areas are very differently regulated within the Community: some Member States prohibit advertising by the legal and medical professions, others allow it; national rules differ in their treatment of unfair competition; some Member States prohibit certain forms of advertising aimed at children; others strictly regulate promotional offers; junk e-mail is subject to conflicting court decisions and statutes throughout the Community. Finally, national rules relating to transparency, i.e. notifying the existence and origin of a commercial communication, are "vague and very divergent" according to the Draft Directive.[16]

The Draft Directive provides that commercial communications must comply with the following conditions:

"(a) the commercial communication must be clearly identifiable as such;
 (b) the natural or legal person on whose behalf the commercial communication is made must be clearly identifiable;
 (c) promotional offers, such as discounts, premiums and gifts, where authorised, must be clearly identifiable as such, and the conditions which must be met to receive them must be easily accessible and be presented accurately and unequivocally;
 (d) promotional competitions or games, where authorised, must be clearly identifiable as such, and the conditions for participation must be easily accessible and be presented accurately and unequivocally". (Article 6)

The Draft Directive expands on the meaning of "identifiable" as used in Articles 6(a) and 6(b). As an example of an identified commercial communication it gives that of a header on a webpage which is clearly labelled; examples given of "hidden" communications include that of an article praising a product which gives no indication that it was commissioned and financed by the product's manufacturer, and that of a site which is silent about the fact that it is entirely sponsored by a private interest for the purpose of advertising.[17] Despite the Draft Directive's guidelines the effectiveness of the provisions relating to the transparency of commercial communications may be limited as it will be difficult for regulators to find out who financed any particular research or website.

---

[14] At 20.
[15] At 11.
[16] At 10.
[17] At 20.

Promotional offers (excluding gambling)[18] can be used to sell goods and services, as long as they are transparent. The Draft Directive suggests that hyper-linked webpage icons[19] will be sufficient to identify those for whom communications are made and to satisfy the requirement to provide easy access to the conditions of promotional offers.[20]

Unsolicited commercial communications are not prohibited by the Draft Directive, which merely provides that they should be clearly and unequivocally identifiable as such as soon as they are received. In terms of e-mail this is likely to mean the marking of the header with some word which indicates its nature. This is somewhat unsatisfactory from the point of view of the individual, in view of the increasing nuisance which unsolicited advertising presents.[21] The Directives on distance contracts[22] and data protection in telecoms[23] prohibit the sending of unsolicited faxes and calls by automatic dialling machines, but not junk e-mail. Member States can derogate from the provisions on unsolicited communications contained in the Draft Directive (see section 3.6 below). Under the Direct Marketing Act 1997 it is currently unlawful in Germany to send unsolicited messages to private persons or households, whether by fax, post, e-mail or telephone, and the Act empowers the courts to issue injunctions against those sending such messages.[24] Although it may be argued that it is an appropriate role for providers of e-mail services to block unsolicited communications where the recipient so requests, this currently presents technical difficulties.

It is unclear how the Draft Directive fits with the Directive on misleading advertising (discussed in Chapter 7 below), which is a measure of minimum harmonisation. It would appear that the Draft Directive contradicts the minimal clause of that Directive. These provisions of the Draft Directive are thus likely to prove controversial, particularly as they permit promotional offers and competitions, and provide no special protection for children.

The Draft Directive makes special provision for commercial communications by "regulated professions", providing that the Member States shall lay down in their legislation that the provision of information society services is authorised given that:

> "the professional rules regarding the independence, dignity and honour of the profession, professional secrecy and fairness towards clients and other members of the profession are met" (Article 8(1)).

[18] Excluded from the scope of the Draft Directive by Article 22(1).
[19] i.e. icons which, when "clicked on", transfer the reader to the "linked" page.
[20] At 20.
[21] Compare the Community position with the Virginia Computer Crimes Act 1998, under which it is a crime to send unsolicited mass e-mails.
[22] Directive 97/7/EC, Article 10. See further Chapter 9 below.
[23] Directive 97/66/EEC, Article 12 prohibits direct marketing by ACMs or fax except where there is prior consent.
[24] For example the case of *Urteil*, where the Langericht Traunstein imposed an injunction against an advertiser who was illegally sending unsolicited commercial messages to a private e-mail address, <www.rhrz.uni-bonn.de/~usa000/urteil.html>. For a list of cases from around the world on junk e-mail see <www.junkemail.org/lawsuits/>.

The reference to "the professional rules" in Article 8(1) relates to the rules of the state in which the professional is based.[25] Whilst Article 8(1) regulates the general use of commercial communications by the regulated professions, Article 8(2) regulates the content of services provided electronically, providing that Member States and the Commission will encourage professional associations to establish codes of conduct at Community level in order to determine the types of information that can be given in commercial communications. Article 8(3) provides the Commission with a power to stipulate what this information should be, "where necessary to ensure the proper functioning of the internal market".[26]

3.3 ELECTRONIC CONTRACTS

Currently, there is doubt about whether the laws of a number of Member States allow for the validity of electronic contracts, both generally and in specific situations. The Draft Directive provides for the generalised validity of electronic contracts:

> "Member States shall ensure that their legislation allows contracts to be concluded electronically. Member States shall in particular ensure that the legal requirements applicable to the contractual process neither prevent the effective use of electronic contracts nor result in such contracts being deprived of legal validity because of the fact that they have been concluded electronically" (Article 9).

Article 9 complements the Commission's recent legislative initiative on a common framework for electronic signatures[27] and requires Member States to carry out a systematic review of those rules which might prevent, limit or deter the use of electronic contracts.[28] Its push towards "equal treatment" for users of paper and electronic media is in line with the UNCITRAL Model Law on Electronic Commerce.[29] The types of rules identified are those relating to all stages of the contractual process, including invitation to treat, offer, acceptance, registration, cancellation, invoicing, and archiving. This will affect requirements for there to be "writing", "an original copy", and for contracts to be "printed" or "published." Finally, requirements relating to physical presence will have to be amended. These requirements might relate to the parties being simultaneously present, or for a contract to be concluded in a particular place, or for a contract to be prepared in the presence of witnesses. The Draft Directive allows Member States to derogate from the generality of Article 9 in respect of

[25] Draft Directive at 21.

[26] Through the advisory committee referred to in Article 23, discussed in s. 3.7 below.

[27] See further, Chapter 4 below, although it is worth emphasising here that "electronic signature" refers to encryption rather than to electronic copies of hand-written signatures.

[28] Draft Directive at 21.

[29] United Nations, *Guide to Enactment of the UNCITRAL Model Law on Electronic Commerce* (1996), Section 6.

contracts requiring the intervention of a notary, those requiring public registration, those involving family law, and those involving the law of succession.[30] It should be noted in the case of consumer contracts that the provisions of the Draft Directive are designed to apply alongside the Directive on distance contracts, discussed in Chapter 9 below.

The Draft Directive lays down detailed rules as to when electronic contracts are concluded. Save as otherwise agreed by professional parties:

"(a) the contract is concluded when the recipient of the service:
—has received from the service provider, electronically, an acknowledgement of receipt of the recipient's acceptance, and
—has confirmed receipt of the acknowledgement of receipt;
(b) acknowledgement of receipt is deemed to be received and confirmation is deemed to have been given when the parties to whom they are addressed are able to access them" (Article 11(1)).[31]

A practical example will help to clarify this difficult provision.[32] Someone called John Dickie buys a book from XYZ Internet Bookstore. He fills in the Web order form and then "submits" it via a mouse click. XYZ Internet Bookstore then informs John, "we have received your acceptance, please click on the button below to confirm that you wish to proceed". John then clicks on the button *and when the website registers the click* (i.e. the service provider is thus able to access the "confirmation"), *the contract is concluded*. The purpose of this circuitous provision appears to be to minimise the possibility of communication breakdown in the contracting process.[33] It also ensures that recipients have time to think twice before irrevocably accepting any offer. Jurisdiction over such contracts made by consumers would appear to lie, under the Brussels Convention, in the state of the consumer's domicile.[34]

---

[30] Article 9(2).

[31] Contrast the Vienna Convention on Contracts for the International Sale of Goods (1980), Article 18(2): "An acceptance of an offer becomes effective at the moment the indication of assent reaches the offeror". See further, "Reconciliation of Legal Traditions in the UN Convention on Contracts for the International Sale of Goods", (1989) 23 *International Law* 443. Taking the same position are the American Bar Association's Model Agreement on Electronic Data Interchange, s.2(1) and §63 of the Restatement (Second) of Contracts (Article 18(2)), and the UNCITRAL Model Law, Article 11.

[32] An example within the Draft Directive or Explanatory Memorandum would have been helpful! In *Commission v Germany* Case C-96/95 [1997] ECR I-1653 the Court ruled that Member State implementation must "guarantee the full application of the directive in a sufficiently clear and precise manner so that, where the directive is intended to create rights for individuals, the persons concerned can ascertain the full extent of their rights" (at 1654). It is questionable whether this provision of the Draft Directive implemented word-for-word could be considered "clear and precise".

[33] Certainty was also why the rule that contractual offers could be accepted by the *posting* of an acceptance was adopted in the English case of *Adams v Lindsell* (1818) 1 B. & Ald 681.

[34] It is submitted that the Convention's requirement for consumers to take all necessary steps to form the contract in the state of their domicile is satisfied in Web contracts of the type exemplified above despite the fact that the Draft Directive states that the confirmation in particular is deemed to be given when the recipient is able to access it. See further Chapter 8.4.1 below.

Article 11(1) only attempts to deal with the situation where the recipient of the service has a concrete offer from the service provider. The situation where it is the recipient who makes the offer is not dealt with and will thus fall to be dealt with by national law, creating the potentially confusing situation of differential treatment of superficially similar contracts.

3.4 LIABILITY OF INTERMEDIARIES

The Draft Directive limits the liability (other than for injunctive relief)[35] of "mere conduits" of information services for the content of those services. This applies in particular to telecoms organisations who provide the information society infrastructure and Internet service providers who host websites. It should be stressed that these provisions do not seek to alter relevant substantive national law. If the service provider does not qualify for the exemption from liability, then that law will still apply.

The general exemption from liability for mere transmission of information will only apply where the provider:

"—does not initiate the transmission,
—does not select the receiver of the transmission, and
—docs not select and does not modify the information contained in the transmission" (Article 12(1)).

Service providers are further exempted from liability where they simply temporarily store or "cache" information (Article 13). "Caching" is the intermediate storage of information for the purpose of speeding information flows. For example, if John Dickie accesses a site in the USA from the University of Warwick, the server in Warwick will typically store all information which John accesses for a temporary period, usually about an hour. Thus, if John wants to access the information again within the hour, the "cache" will greatly reduce the time taken to do this. There are some exceptions to this general exclusion of liability for caching, the most important of which is where the provider does not act expeditiously to remove or to disable access to information upon obtaining actual knowledge that a competent authority has ordered such action (Article 13 (e)).

The Draft Directive contains similar provision on "hosting".[36] A typical "hosting" situation is where a company such as VirginNet hires Web space to an individual. The individual can then freely put information on the Web. VirginNet "hosts" the information, but will generally not attempt to control what the individual puts on the site.

---

[35] The provisions limiting the liability of intermediaries for transmission, caching, and hosting are all subject to the provisions relating to injunctive relief contained in Article 18, discussed in section 3.5 below.

[36] Article 14.

Thus "host" service providers are exempted from liability, except for injunctive relief, for information stored at the request of the recipient of the service provided that:

> "—the provider does not have actual knowledge that the activity is illegal and, as regards claims for damages, is not aware of facts or circumstances from which illegal activity is apparent; or
> —the provider, upon obtaining such knowledge or awareness, acts expeditiously to remove or to disable access to the information" (Article 14(1)).

Thus, service providers will generally not be liable under the criminal or civil law for the contents of websites, bulletin board systems, or newsgroups which they host. However, a duty to be vigilant is imposed on service providers. The Draft Directive states that the Commission is actively encouraging the establishment of self-regulatory systems, including codes of conduct and telephone hotlines.[37] The final provision relating to the liability of intermediaries is the prohibition of national measures obliging providers to screen or monitor third party content. This is without prejudice to any "targeted, temporary surveillance activities required by national judicial authorities in accordance with national legislation to safeguard national security, defence, public security and for the prevention, investigation, detection and prosecution of criminal offences".[38]

3.5 IMPLEMENTATION AND ENFORCEMENT

The Draft Directive contains extensive provision on enforcement and implementation. The Commission and the Member States are to encourage the development of codes of conduct at Community level.[39] Provision is made to encourage the parties involved to send draft national codes to the Commission so that an assessment may be made of their compatibility with Community law.[40] However, it is not clear whether codes of conduct will prove a sufficiently powerful tool to control suppliers in any meaningful way, or with any consistency across the Community. The Draft Directive does not tie the codes into any binding legal framework. Research has shown that codes of conduct can be

---

[37] See generally: Commission Communication, *An Action Plan on Promoting Safe Use of the Internet* (COM(97) 582). See also Council Recommendation 98/560 on the development of the competitiveness of the European audio-visual and information services industry by promoting national frameworks aimed at achieving a comparable and effective level of protection of minors and human dignity, OJ 1998 L270/48.

[38] Article 15.

[39] Article 16.

[40] Article 16(b). See also Directive 98/34/EC, OJ 1998 L204/37, as amended by Directive 98/48/EC, OJ 1998 L217/18, which provides that voluntary agreements to which a public authority is party must be notified in accordance with the terms of the Directive.

ineffective in large, disparate markets with low entry barriers,[41] and the electronic marketplace is a good example of such.

Further to promoting the development of Community codes of conduct, the Draft Directive also provides that effective out of court dispute settlement mechanisms must be available under national legislation.[42] In line with the Commission Recommendation on the principles applicable to the bodies responsible for out of court settlement of consumer disputes,[43] the Draft Directive lays down certain principles for these bodies:

> "Member States shall ensure that bodies responsible for out of court settlement of consumer disputes apply the principles of independence and transparency, the adversarial principle, and the principles of effectiveness of procedure, legality of the decision, liberty of parties and representation" (Article 19(1)).

Out of court dispute settlement mechanisms are particularly valuable in the context of low-value transactions where one party is significantly more powerful than the other.[44] In these cases, the prospect of expensive and time-consuming court action can intimidate those with limited resources and prevent the resolution of the dispute. The Draft Directive's insistence on the availability of effective out of court mechanisms is a positive development from the point of view of individuals in particular.

The Draft Directive also contains more generalised enforcement provision. In recognition of the fact that rapid action will often be necessary to stop unlawful activity in the information society, it provides:

> "Member States shall ensure that effective actions can be brought against information society services' activities by allowing measures to be taken as rapidly as possible by way of interim injunctions in order to remedy an alleged infringement and to protect the interested parties from being subject to further damages" (Article 18(1)).

Article 18(1) facilitates rapid reaction to alleged unlawful activity. Article 18(2) goes on to provide that acts in breach of national rules incorporating Articles 5 to 15 (information requirements, commercial communications, electronic contracts, and liability of intermediaries) are to be considered as infringements within the meaning of Article 1(2) of the Directive on cross-border injunctions.[45]

The Draft Directive's final substantive provision relating to enforcement is contained in Article 19 which obliges Member States to ensure that their competent authorities are adequately equipped to deal effectively and rapidly both with individuals and with corresponding authorities elsewhere in the

---

[41] European Consumer Law Group, "Non-Legislative Means of Consumer Protection", (1983) 6 JCP 209.

[42] Article 17.

[43] 98/257/EC, contained in COM(98) 198.

[44] See further Draft Directive at 30.

[45] Directive 98/27/EC. Article 1(2) allows cross-border applications for injunctions against activity breaching Community consumer law, see further Chapter 8 below.

Community. Member States must ensure that their authorities are able to provide information relating to contractual rights and obligations, the co-ordinates of other relevant authorities, and to assist parties in cases of dispute.[46] The Commission, guided by an Advisory Committee, is granted the power to determine the rules governing this co-operation between national authorities.[47]

3.6 DEROGATIONS

Three types of derogation from the generality of the Draft Directive are provided, in order to imbue its exceptionally wide-ranging provisions with some flexibility.[48]

First, Article 22(1) excludes the areas of taxation and protection of personal data. Fiscal issues in electronic commerce are under review in the work launched by the Commission Communication, *Electronic Commerce and Indirect Taxation*.[49] Data protection is considered to have been exhaustively regulated by Directive 95/46.[50] Further, Article 22(1) excludes from the Draft Directive, on the basis of the current lack of harmonisation in the relevant areas,[51] amongst other things, the activities of notaries, the representation of a client and defence of his interests before the courts, and gambling activities, excluding those carried out for commercial communications purposes.[52] This list can be amended by the Commission in accordance with the Advisory Committee procedure detailed in section 3.7 below.

Secondly, Member States are permitted to derogate from the internal market clause of the Draft Directive[53] in the following areas (Annex II, footnotes included):

"—copyright, neighbouring rights, rights referred to in Directive 87/54/EEC[54] and Directive 96/9/EEC[55] as well as industrial property rights;
—the emission of electronic money by institutions in respect of which Member States have applied one of the derogations provided for in Article 7(1) of Directive 000/00/EC;[56]

[46] Article 19(4).
[47] Article 19(6). See further on the Advisory Committee, section 3.7 below.
[48] Draft Directive at 26.
[49] COM(98) 374.
[50] Directive 95/46/EC of the European Parliament and of the Council on the protection of individuals with regard to the processing of personal data and on the free movement of such data, OJ 1995 L281/31. See further, Chapter 6 below.
[51] Draft Directive at 27.
[52] Annex I.
[53] Article 3.
[54] Council Directive of 16 December 1986 on the legal protection of typographies of semiconductor products, OJ 1987 L24 L24/36–40.
[55] Directive of the European Parliament and of the Council of 11 March 1996 on the legal protection of databases, OJ 1996 L77/20–28.
[56] Proposal for a Directive . . ./. . ./EC amending Directive 77/780/EC on the co-ordination of laws, regulations and administrative provisions relating to the taking up and pursuit of the business of credit institutions (COM(98) 727).

—Article 44 paragraph 2 of Directive 85/611/EEC;[57]
—Article 30 and Title V of Directive 92/49/EEC,[58] Title IV of Directive 92/96/EEC,[59] Article 7 and 8 of Directive 88/357/EEC [60] and Article 4 of Directive 90/619/EEC;[61]
—contractual obligations concerning consumer contracts
—unsolicited commercial communications by electronic mail, or by an equivalent individual communication".

The Commission has stated that these areas are excluded because within them:

"it is *impossible to apply the principle of mutual recognition* as set out in the case law of the Court of Justice concerning the principles of freedom of movement enshrined in the Treaty, or it is an area where mutual recognition cannot be achieved and there is *insufficient harmonisation* to guarantee an equivalent level of protection between Member States, there are *provisions laid down by existing Directives which are clearly incompatible* with Article 3 because they explicitly require supervision in the country of destination".[62]

Thirdly, the Draft Directive provides for derogation from the general (Article 3(2)) obligation on Member States not to restrict information society services from another Member State. This derogation is contained within Article 22(3) and applies without prejudice to court actions. It only applies where the derogation is consistent with Community law, is proportionate, and is necessary for one of the following reasons:

"—public policy, in particular the protection of minors, or the fight against any incitement to hatred on grounds of race, sex, religion or nationality,
—the protection of public health,
—public security,
—consumer protection".[63]

Measures taken under Article 22(3) must further be taken in respect of services which prejudice the above objectives or which present a serious and grave

---

[57] Council Directive of 20 December 85 on the co-ordination of laws, regulations and administrative provisions relating to undertaking for collective investment in transferable securities (UCITS), OJ 1985 L375/3–18.

[58] Council Directive of 18 June 1992 on the co-ordination of laws, regulations and administrative provisions relating to direct insurance other than life assurance and amending Directives 73/239/EEC and 88/357/EEC (third non-life insurance Directive), OJ 1992 L228/1–23.

[59] Council Directive of 10 November 1992 on the co-ordination of laws, regulations and administrative provisions relating to direct life insurance and amending Directives 79/267/EEC and 90/619/EEC (third life assurance Directive), OJ 1992 L360/1–27.

[60] Second Council Directive 88/357/EEC of 22 June 1988 on the co-ordination of laws, regulations and administrative provisions relating to direct insurance other than life assurance and laying down provisions to facilitate the effective exercise of freedom to provide services and amending Directive 73/239/EEC, OJ 1988 L172/1–14.

[61] Council Directive of 8 November 1990 on the co-ordination of laws, regulations and administrative provisions relating to direct life assurance laying down provisions to facilitate the effective exercise of freedom to provide services and amending Directive 79/267/EEC, OJ 1990 L330/50–61.

[62] Draft Directive at 32. Italics in original.

[63] Article 22(3)(a)(i).

risk of prejudice to those objectives. Thus, Member States must show good cause for relevant derogation and are prohibited from adopting sweeping measures which do not sufficiently target manifest problems. Further, Member States wishing to use the Article 22(3) derogation must, except in emergency cases, request and allow time for the "home" Member State to take effective measures, and, in the event of inadequate action, notify the Commission and the Member State of its intention to apply the derogation prior to so doing.[64] The Commission may rule on the compatibility of national measures with Community law.[65]

3.7 THE ADVISORY COMMITTEE

The Draft Directive provides for an Advisory Committee to assist the Commission in the exercise of its enforcement powers.[66] The Committee is to consist of representatives of the Member States and be chaired by a representative of the Commission. The Commission is not bound by the Advisory Committee's opinion but is to "take the utmost account" of it, which indicates that quite exceptional reasons must exist (and in line with the principle of transparency, be given) for the Commission to depart from the Committee's opinion.

[64] Articles 22(3)(b), (c).
[65] In accordance with the procedure outlined is section 3.7 below.
[66] Article 23.

4

Cryptography and the Draft Directive on Electronic Signatures

An adequate legal framework for electronic signatures is widely seen as an essential factor in the development of electronic commerce. In business conducted at a distance, electronic signatures can guarantee the identity of the parties as well as the integrity and confidentiality[1] of messages. Traditionally, both business practice and the law have required commercial agreements to be evidenced. The reasons for this lie in the desire both to ensure certainty and to satisfy the demands of public authorities such as those involved in the collection of taxes and customs duties. Needs for certainty and accountability also press upon electronic commerce.[2] There may be solutions to the problem of ensuring certainty which can be gleaned from applying existing law to electronic commerce, but it is clear from relevant legislative activity throughout the Member States that existing law does not satisfactorily deal with electronic signatures. A reasonable level of legal uniformity seems to be a realistic possibility in view of the fact that the issue is so new. Countries can approach the issue without historical ties. Although Electronic Data Interchange has been used in business for some time without the framework of specific law (a number of *non-binding* instruments have been issued),[3] the more open, global and anonymous nature of the Internet has created a demand for specific law.

4.1 FUNCTIONING OF ELECTRONIC SIGNATURES[4]

An electronic signature is a software-driven method of authenticating the origin and integrity of an electronic message. An electronic signature is in no way a

---

[1] Privacy considerations raised by cryptography will not be detailed in this chapter, detail can be found in: Y Akdeniz *et al*, "Cryptography and Liberty: Can the Trusted Third Parties be Trusted? A Critique of the Recent UK Proposals," (1997)2 *JILT* <http://elj.warwick.ac.uk/jilt/cryp tog/97_2akdz/>; E. Szafran, "Regulatory issues raised by cryptography on the Internet", (1998) 3 *Communications Law* 38; B. Koops, "A Survey of Cryptography Laws and Regulations", (1996) 12 *CLSR* 349.

[2] One survey found that while 53% of Internet users had used the Internet to reach a decision on a purchase, only 15% of those had made that purchase online: *The Economist*, 10 May 1997. There is no doubt that even sophisticated computer networks are susceptible to fraud—in 1998, Citibank were defrauded of $2.8 million by a computer hacker, *Financial Times*, 18 August 1995.

[3] In particular, Commission Recommendation 94/820/EC relating to the legal aspects of electronic data interchange, OJ 1994 L338/98, which contains the European Model EDI Agreement.

[4] See generally: Computer Science and Telecommunications Board United States National

manipulation of a hand-written signature. It is a sequence of bits generated by a mathematical function creating a message digest. The sender's public and private keys are then put through the digest and a unique data-string is created. A recipient who has the sender's public key can determine whether the message was created using the private key corresponding to that public key and whether the message has been altered since originally scrambled into a data-string. Each electronic signature is unique to the message to which it is attached. The keys are transportable between messages, the signature is not.

The sender's public key will generally be available to anyone who wants it, via the sender's website for example, or via a repository maintained by a provider of keys. Once obtained it can be used to decrypt any message from that sender. Provided that the decryption does not produce an unintelligible string of characters, the recipient will be assured of the origin and integrity of the message.

The utility of electronic signatures is dependent upon the recipient knowing that the public key he holds is truly that of the sender. There exists a danger that a fraudster might post a false public key on a publicly accessible database. One method of ensuring that a public key is that of a particular sender is through the use of a trusted third party or certification authority as intermediary, a bank or a postal service for example.[5] As will be seen below, the Commission has proposed a system of "Certification Service Providers" as the European solution to this problem.

4.2 DRAFT DIRECTIVE ON ELECTRONIC SIGNATURES

The Community's first steps towards regulating electronic signatures were taken in the Commission's 1997 Communication, *A European Initiative in Electronic Commerce*, which emphasised the need for legislation.[6] This initiative was followed by the Commission Communication, *Towards a European Framework for Digital Signatures and Encryption*,[7] and subsequently its *Proposal for a European Parliament and Council Directive on a common framework for electronic signatures*[8] ("the Draft Directive"). As its title suggests, the

Research Council, *Cryptography's Role in Securing the Information Society* (Washington DC, National Academy Press, 1996); United States National Institute of Standards and Technology Computer Security Resource Clearinghouse, *Cryptography FAQ: Public Key Cryptography*, <http://csrc.ncsl.nist.gov/nistpubs/800–2.txt>; M. Baum, "Digital Signature Technical Primer in Verisign, Inc., Notarial FAQ: Frequently Asked Questions" <http://www.verisign.com/repository/notryfaq.html>.

[5] See for example, <www.usps.gov>, detailing the US Postal Service's role as a certification authority. The USPS photographs and fingerprints all those who request certification of their signatures.

[6] COM(97) 157, at III.

[7] COM(97) 503.

[8] COM(98) 297. The European Parliament adopted a favourable opinion on the Draft Directive on 16 December 1998, *Report on Proposal for a European Parliament and Council Directive on a*

Draft Directive does not aim to provide a singular law, but a legal framework for Member States to work within. This approach is designed to accomodate the dynamism of electronic signature technology and is similar to that already adopted in the field by various European and non-European countries,[9] and international organisations.[10] Of course, in contrast to the international instruments, the Draft Directive contains a binding framework.[11]

Many individual Member States have, or are preparing, legislation on electronic signatures, as Table 4.1 indicates. The national initiatives there detailed take divergent approaches to the conditions under which electronic signatures have legal effect, the structure of accreditation schemes, the liability of certification service providers, and jurisdiction over cross-border disputes.[12] The Draft Directive aims to minimise the barriers to cross-border trade which these differences might throw up. It makes provision, in accordance with the principle of mutual recognition, for the Community-wide validity of certificates issued in the Member States, thus stimulating a single market for certification service providers.[13] Annexes 1 and 2 establish essential requirements for certificates and certification service providers. Certificates are required, amongst other things, to identify the provider, the unmistakable name or pseudonym of the holder, a specific attribute of the holder (such as the address or the authority to act on behalf of a company) and a signature verification device which corresponds to a signature creation device under the control of the holder. Certification service providers are required, amongst other things, to demonstrate the reliability necessary for offering certification services, to operate a prompt revocation service, to verify the identity and capacity to act of holders, to maintain sufficient financial resources to bear the risk of liability for damages, and to inform consumers of the terms and conditions in writing and plain language before entering into a contractual relationship.

common framework for electronic signatures (A4–0507/98). As a note on the discrepancy in terminology, the Draft Directive refers to "electronic" signatures, whilst the earlier Communication refers to "digital" signatures because the Draft Directive is designed to fit technologies which have not yet been developed (Recital 6). However, the change is a departure from standard terminology and has come in for criticism, see A. Kelman, "Just say 'non' ", (1998)3 *JILT* <http://www.law.warwick.ac.uk/jilt/98-3/>.

[9] For example, Germany's Digital Signature Act 1997 states as its objective, "to establish general conditions under which digital signatures are deemed secure and forgeries of digital signatures or manipulation of signed data can be reliably ascertained". American policy is to encourage the development of a voluntary, market-driven key management system: White House Information Infrastructure Task Force, *A Framework for Global Electronic Commerce*, <http://www.iitf.nist.gov/>, at II(6).

[10] ICC guidelines at <http://www.iccwbo.org/guidec2.htm>; OECD Ottawa Conference on Electronic Commerce, "Ministerial Declaration on Authentication for Electronic Commerce", (DSTI/ICCP/REG(98)9/REV4) at <http://www.ottawaoecdconference.org/>; UNCITRAL Draft Uniform Rules on Electronic Signatures (Working Group paper A/CN.9/WG.IV/WP.79), <www.un.or.at/uncitral/english/sessions/wg_ec/wp-79.htm>.

[11] Under Article 249 of the EC Treaty, Directives are binding as to the result to be achieved. Instruments adopted by bodies such as the ICC and UNCITRAL are entirely non-binding.

[12] Draft Directive at 5.

[13] Article 4.

Table 4.1: Legislation on electronic signatures in Member States
Source: Draft Directive at 4-5

Member State	Status of legislative initiatives
Austria	• Preparatory work.
Belgium	• Telecommunications law: voluntary prior declaration scheme for service providers. • Drafting of law on certification services related to digital signatures. • Drafting of law amending the Civil Code with regard to electronic evidence. • Drafting of law on the use of digital signatures in social security and public health.
Denmark	• Drafting of law on the secure and efficient use of digital communications.
France	• Telecommunications Law (Authorization and Exemption Decrees): —supply of electronic signature products and services subject to information procedure. —use, import and export of electronic signature products and services free. • Legislation concerning the use of digital signatures in social security and public health.
Finland	• Drafting of law on the electronic exchange of information in administration and administrative judicial procedures. • Drafting on law on the status of the Population Register Centre as provider of certification services.
Germany	• Digital signature law and ordinance in place: conditions under which digital signatures are deemed secure; voluntary accreditation of service providers. • Drafting of catalogue of suitable security measures. • Public consultation on legal aspects of digital signatures and digitally signed electronic documents currently ongoing.
Italy	• General law on the reform of the public service and administrative simplification in place: principle of legal recognition of electronic documents. • Decree on creation, archiving and transmission of electronic documents and contracts. • Decree on requirements on products and services under preparation. • Decree on the fiscal obligations arising from electronic documents under preparation.
Netherlands	• Voluntary accreditation scheme for service providers in preparation.

Member State	Status of legislative initiatives
	• Taxation law providing for the electronic filing of income statements.
	• Draft law amending the Civil Code under preparation.
Spain	• Circulars of the customs department on the use of electronic signatures.
	• Resolution in the field of social security regulating the use of electronic means.
	• Laws and circulars in the field of mortgages, taxation, financial services and registration of enterprises allowing the use of electronic procedures.
	• Budget Law 1998 mandating the Mint to act as a certification service provider.
Sweden	• Preparatory work.
United Kingdom	• Drafting of legislation concerning the voluntary licensing of certification service providers and the legal recognition of electronic signatures.

Member States are obliged to ensure that an electronic signature is not denied legal effect solely on the ground that it is in electronic form, and that certified electronic signatures are recognised as satisfying any legal requirement of a hand-written signature.[14] In order to promote trust the Draft Directive establishes a basic rule that certification service providers shall be liable for their certificates to anyone who reasonably relies upon them.[15]

Criteria are set out for the recognition of certificates originating in non-Member States, namely (Article 7(1)):

"(a) if the certification service provider fulfils the requirements laid down in this Directive and has been accredited in the context of a voluntary accreditation scheme established by a Member State; or

(b) if a certification service provider established within the Community, which fulfils the requirements laid down in Annex II guarantees the certificate to the same extent as its own certificates; or

(c) if the certificate of the certification service provider is recognized under the regime of a bilateral or multilateral agreement between the Community and third countries or international organizations".[16]

---

[14] Article 5.

[15] Article 6. There are certain qualifications to this rule, including one permitting certification service providers to indicate in the certificate a limit on the value of transactions for which the certificate is valid (Article 6(4)).

[16] Compare the German Digital Signature Act 1997, s. 15: "digital signatures capable of being verified by a public signature key certified in another Member State of the EU (or of) the European

The Community is here concerned not to obstruct the development of an international framework for electronic signatures. The criteria set out for the validation of third country certificates are not onerous. In particular, in view of the commercial interest in providing global certification services, third country service providers are likely to find it easy to have their certificates validated through partnerships with Community providers under Article 7(1)(b).

Reflecting the fact that electronic signature technology is subject to rapid change, the Draft Directive provides for the Commission to establish and publish reference numbers of generally recognised standards for electronic signature products.[17] In respect of products which meet a generally recognised standard, Member States are to presume that the signature is trustworthy.[18] In establishing standards, the Commission is to consult the Electronic Signature Committee, composed of representatives of the Member States and chaired by a representative of the Commission.[19]

The Draft Directive is, in line with the OECD and UNCITRAL developments cited above, technology-neutral and does not focus upon any particular kind of electronic signature. Currently, the most commonly-used type of electronic signature is public-key cryptography, but there is no guarantee that this will be the case in the future. The Draft Directive is designed to be applicable to technologies which have not yet been developed.[20] With the same rationale, the Draft Directive provides that Member States shall not make the provision of certification services subject to prior authorisation.[21]

The Draft Directive does not deal with criminal-law-related issues of electronic signatures, although the Commission has produced a study on this topic.[22] Further, the Council of Europe in 1995 adopted a Recommendation concerning problems of criminal procedural law connected to information

---

Economic Area shall be deemed equivalent to digital signatures under this Act insofar as they show the same level of security" (within Article 3 of the Federal Act Establishing the General Conditions for Information and Communication Services).

[17]   Article 3(3).

[18]   Ibid. The standard for trustworthiness is laid down in Annex II(e): certification service providers must "use trustworthy systems, and use electronic signature products that ensure protection against modification of the products so that they cannot be used to perform functions other than those for which they have been designed; they must also use electronic signature products that ensure the technical and cryptographic security of the certification processes supported by the products".

[19]   Article 9.

[20]   Anxiety to ensure that the Directive is "future-proof" might explain why the Community has been slow in comparison to other legislative bodies in bringing legislation forward. An example of hasty legislation causing problems is the Utah Digital Signature Act 1995, which although it provided for the establishment of certification authorities, lacked clarity to the extent that the first such authority was not set up until late-1997 (Report of the Electronic Commerce Expert Group to the Australian Attorney General, "Electronic Commerce: Building the Legal Framework", March 1998, <http://law.gov.au/aghome/advisory/eceg/single.htm#> at 14). For a US example of technology-neutral legislation, see California's statute, California Government Code §16.5(a).

[21]   Article 3(1).

technology and Explanatory Memorandum.[23] Nor does the Draft Directive prejudice the competence of the Union and Member States to regulate the export of cryptography.[24] Both the European Union[25] and individual Member States[26] have acted to restrict the export of cryptography. These restrictions have been established to comply with the Treaty of the Co-ordinating Committee for Multilateral Export Controls (COCOM), and the subsequent Wassenaar Arrangement on Export Controls for Conventional Arms and Dual-Use Goods and Technologies (July 1996).[27] It is questionable whether these export restrictions will achieve their ends for two reasons. First, it is simple to export cryptography surreptitiously, as it can be done via a telephone line. Secondly, most of the regulations are based on computing power[28] and thus become outdated quickly, as the power used will constantly increase in line with computing power generally. These complications are manifested in the fact that some countries apply *import* restrictions in order that their existing regulatory regimes are not distorted by sudden changes in available cryptography.[29]

Given the European Parliament's favourable report, cited above, it can be expected that the Draft Directive will be adopted at some point in 1999. The Draft Directive provides for Member States to implement it by 31 December 2000.[30]

[22] Project Aequitas, "The admission as evidence in trials of penal character of electronic documents signed digitally", <http://aequitas.encomix.es/infofi2i.htm>.

[23] R 95(13) (Council of Europe, Strasbourg, 1995). See also: Recommendation 89(9) on computer related crime (Council of Europe, Strasbourg, 1995); I. Carr and K. Williams, "Council of Europe on the Harmonisation of Criminal Procedural Laws Relating to Information Technology (Recommendation No. R95(13))—Some Comments", [1998] *JBL* 468.

[24] Recital 7.

[25] All Member States are bound by Council Regulation 3381/94/EC, made pursuant to Council Decision 941/942 CFSP.

[26] For example: the United Kingdom's Export of Goods (Control) Order 1989, SI 1989/2376; Article 17 of the French Telecommunications Act of 26 July 1996, No. 96–659, *Journel Officiel*, 27 July 1996, English translation at <www.telecom.gouv.fr/english/activ/telecom/nloi17.htm>.

[27] "Dual-use goods and technologies"refers to those which can be used for both military and civil purposes, and includes cryptography.

[28] See for example, Article 17 of the French Telecommunications Act of 26 July 1996; Article 5 of the Edict of Boris Yeltsin of 3 April 1995, "On Actions for Preserving Lawfulness in the Field of Development, Manufacturing, Sale and Use of Encryption Devices and on Providing Services Related to Data Encryption", <www.nww.com/ruscrypto.html>; Department of Commerce, Encryption Export Regulations, Federal Register, 30 December 1996, vol. 61, no. 251 (at the moment export and re-export of keys up to 56 bits are permitted).

[29] For example France, see note 27 above.

[30] Article 13(1).

5

Copyright

5.1 INTRODUCTION

Electronic commerce poses fresh problems for the law of intellectual property in general and copyright in particular.[1] Digital technology provides new possibilities for copying and distribution. Digital copies are of identical quality to the original and are cheap to produce. Mass distribution can occur rapidly and surreptitiously from anywhere in the world. Copyright affects a wide range of works, including computer programs, broadcasts, theatre performances, literature, music, and art. The right-holders concerned include authors, producers, broadcasters, and performers.

The electronic market for copyright goods and services is one of growth,[2] spurred by improvements in quality and in efficiency of reproduction and distribution.[3] As the capacity of both networks and personal computers increases, market growth for electronic copyright material is likely to accelerate.[4] Although offline[5] carrier capacity is currently growing faster than that of online,[6] the ease of online use presages its future dominance. The appropriate regulation of these markets is currently the subject of vigourous debate, in both the Community and the USA.[7]

---

[1] This book does not deal with Community trade mark law (principally Directive 89/104 approximating the laws of Member States relating to trademarks, OJ 1989 L40/1; Council Regulation 40/94 on Community trademarks, as amended by OJ 1994 L349/83, OJ 1994 L11/1) or domain names. Further information on the problems posed by domain names for trade mark law can be found in the Commission Communication, *Globalisation and the Information Society*, *The Need for Strengthened International Co-ordination* (COM(98)50); also Commission, *Issues Involving the Registration of Domain Names* (July 1997), available at <http://www.ispo.cec.be/>. Another summary of the legal issues involved is available on the World Intellectual Property Organisation website, <http://www.wipo.org>.

[2] For example, the electronic information services sector grew by 27% per annum between 1989 and 1994 (*Proposal for a Directive on copyright and related rights in the Information Society* (COM(97) 628), at 4).

[3] For example, digital broadcasting can provide 10 times the number of channels of conventional broadcasting.

[4] To give some idea of current network capacity, transmission of the contents of a CD-ROM over the Internet from the USA to England would take approximately 17 hours.

[5] For example CD-ROMs or video.

[6] For example, the recently-developed Digital Video Disk has a capacity 10 times that of a CD-ROM. Online capacity is of course dependent on networks which are expensive to replace.

[7] See generally, D. Tang and C. Weinstein, "Electronic Commerce: American and International Proposals for Legal Structures", in C. McCrudden (ed), *Regulation and Deregulation: Policy and Practice in the Utilities and Financial Services Industries* (Oxford, Clarendon Press, 1999) at 321.

The market in electronic copyright material is concentrated in the financial, education, information, communication and leisure sectors. Users may call up copyright material for display (e.g. art), or download it (e.g. software). Some of the most popular online copyright material is music which is downloaded, legitimately or illegitimately, by individuals to CD-ROM "burners".[8] This service is available in both Europe[9] and the USA[10] and will no doubt grow exponentially as greater numbers of people gain access to the Internet.

Currently, no Community Law expressly covers "on-demand" transmissions of copyright works, although the following all have some impact on intellectual property in the electronic marketplace:

(1)   Directive 91/250/EEC on the legal protection of computer programs,[11] which extends the protection offered to literary works to computer programs;

(2)   Directive 92/100/EEC on rental right and on lending right and on certain rights related to copyright in the field of intellectual property;[12]

(3)   Directive 93/83/EEC on the co-ordination of certain rules concerning copyright and rights related to copyright applicable to satellite broadcasting and cable retransmission;[13]

(4)   Directive 93/98/EEC harmonising the term of copyright and certain related rights,[14] which defines relevant periods of protection;

(5)   Directive 96/9/EC on the legal protection of databases[15] containing a *sui generis* right providing protection against unauthorised extraction or re-use of the database contents.

The right to communicate protected works to the public has been harmonised in a patchwork fashion by the Directives detailed above. The Computer Programmes Directive 91/250 protects "any form of distribution to the public" (Article 4). The Cable and Satellite Directive 93/83 gives authors an exclusive right of communication to the public of works by satellite and cable retransmission (Article 8). To that list might be added the private international law rules governing copyright infringement, which are discussed in Chapter 8 below. This patchwork of regulation has resulted in demand for a new Community instrument, a draft of which is currently under consideration and this is analysed below.

---

[8]   A burner is currently priced at approximately $200. Downloading a CD-ROM to a burner costs as little as $5 compared to a cost of more than $15 for a CD-ROM from a shop. The quality is identical. Music can also be downloaded without payment from pirate websites.

[9]   "Deutsche Telekom in on-line music link", *Financial Times*, 5 June 1997.

[10]   "US record companies to launch Internet sales drive", *Financial Times*, 7 August 1997.

[11]   OJ 1991 L122/42.

[12]   OJ 1992 L346/61.

[13]   OJ 1993 L248/15.

[14]   OJ 1993 L290/9.

[15]   OJ 1996 L77/20.

5.2 THE DRAFT DIRECTIVE ON COPYRIGHT IN THE INFORMATION SOCIETY

In 1997 the Commission acted to deal with the problems highlighted above by adopting the Draft Directive on the harmonisation of certain aspects of copyright and related rights in the Information Society[16] ("the Draft Directive"). The Draft Directive is a development from the Commission's 1994 Action Plan on the Information Society[17] and its 1995 Green Paper on copyright.[18] It is based on the two World Intellectual Property Organisation Treaties,[19] the WIPO Copyright Treaty 1996 (WCT) and the WIPO Performances and Phonograms Treaty 1996 (WPPT). They contain provisions specifically designed to deal with the problems posed by electronic media.

Community action is proposed on two grounds.[20] First, on the basis that harmonised legal protection will create a level playing field within the internal market, in accordance with the EC Treaty.[21] Authors, right-holders and users would thus know what rules are generally applicable throughout the Community. Secondly, action is proposed on the basis of resolving the uncertainties surrounding the applicability of existing legislation[22] to electronic media.

Both the foundations and the content of copyright law differ amongst the Member States.[23] Although the author's exclusive right of reproduction is important within all Member States' laws, some Member States provide a narrow definition of "reproduction" and it is unclear whether these narrow definitions encompass non-tangible media. There are further differences in respect of exceptions. Some Member States provide exceptions for "fair dealing" and libraries, others do not. The Draft Directive does not attempt to obliterate all

---

[16] Contained in the *Proposal for a Directive on copyright and related rights in the Information Society* (COM(97) 628) ("Proposal"), <http://europa.eu.int/comm/dg15/en/intprop/intprop/index. htm>. Parliament on 10 February 1999 adopted the Report on the Draft Directive of the Committee on Legal Affairs and Citizens' Rights (A4–0026/99) ("the Barzanti Report"). A Council Common Position is expected in the course of 1999.

[17] COM(94) 347.

[18] "Copyright and Related Rights in the Information Society" (COM(95) 382). See also the Parliament's Resolution on the Green Paper (A4–0255/96).

[19] Adopted in Geneva by the Diplomatic Conference on Certain Copyright and Neighbouring Rights Questions on 20 December 1996. The Community has signed these Treaties, although not ratified them (indeed as of February 1999 only two of 50 signatories had ratified them, Belarus and the Moldova Republic. The Treaties and related information can be accessed through <http://www.wipo.int>.

[20] See Proposal, n. 16 above, at 3.

[21] Articles 28 (free movement of goods) and 49 (free movement of services) in particular.

[22] As detailed above, see also the *Proposal for a Directive on the re-sale right for the benefit of the author of an original work of art* (COM(96) 97), OJ 1996 C178.

[23] As regards the foundations of copyright law, one might compare the English "sweat on the brow" test (where there has been sweat, there should be copyright, see *Leslie v Young* [1894] AC 335 involving a railway timetable) with the laws of Continental countries which require some originality in the work. For a comprehensive survey of the approaches of different countries, see International Bureau of WIPO, *Existing international, regional and national legislation concerning the protection of the rights of broadcasting organizations* (SCCR/1/3, September 1998), <http://www.wipo.int/eng/meetings/1998/sccr_98/index.htm>.

the differences in approach between Member States, it is a measure of approximation, not of maximum harmonisation. The full extent to which Member States will be allowed to maintain their own legal and cultural traditions in this area will depend on the European Court's interpretation of any final Directive.

The scope of the Draft Directive is not limited to any particular technology (Article 1). The core right is that of authors to authorise or prohibit reproductions (Article 2). An exclusive right of reproduction is also granted to other right-holders, including performers, phonogram producers, film producers and broadcasters. These right-holders already have an exclusive right of reproduction under Article 7 of the Rental Rights Directive.[24] However, it is unclear how this Article applies to the electronic environment and the Draft Directive deletes it.[25] The field is taken exclusively by Article 2 of the Draft Directive, which clearly does encompass electronic media: it applies to "direct or indirect, temporary or permanent reproduction by any means and in any form, in whole or in part".

The application of Article 2 to "indirect" reproduction refers to a situation such as copying a work of art which has been posted on a web-page. The copying is indirect because of the medium of the web-page, i.e. the original is copied to the web-page which is then itself copied.[26] The words "temporary or permanent" in Article 2 serve to include within its scope the storage of copyright material in a computer, whether in transient memory or on hard disk.

5.2.1 Right of communication to the public

Article 3(1) grants authors the exclusive right to authorise or prohibit any communication to the public, in line with Article 8 WCT. It covers communication to the public "by wire or wireless means, including the making available to the public of their works in such a way that members of the public may access them from a place and at a time individually chosen by them". The concept of "communication to the public" is taken from the Berne Convention[27] and the WCT. The concept of the public choosing the time and place of access is also to be found in Article 8 WCT. Article 3(1) of the Draft Directive is designed to include the situation where unrelated individuals at different times and in different places receive "on-demand" transmissions. There is no need for any member of the public to access copyright material for there to be a breach of Article 3(1), the threshold is crossed simply by making the material available to the public. Use of the term, "public", excludes private communication. The "making avail-

---

[24] Directive 92/100/EEC, OJ 1992 L346/61.

[25] Article 10(1).

[26] The concept of "indirect" copying is also to be found in Article 7 of Directive 92/100 on rental rights and in Article 10 of the Rome Convention for the Protection of Performers, Producers of Phonograms and Broadcasting Organizations 1961.

[27] Berne Convention for the Protection of Literary and Artistic Works 1971, a summary is available at <http://www.wipo.int/eng/iplex/wo_ber0_.htm>.

able" right covers only material made available at a time and from a place chosen by the individual. It does not cover broadcasting or "near-on-demand" services.[28]

Article 3(2) grants relevant exclusive rights to right-holders other than authors, i.e. the right-holders listed in Article 2. Article 3(2) implements Articles 10 and 14 WPPT. Non-interactive transmissions are not covered, leaving related existing provisions (Article 8 Rental Rights Directive, Article 4 Cable Satellite Directive) in place. The scope of Article 3(2) is wider than the WPPT in that it grants the exclusive right of reproduction to all right-holders who already have related rights in the *aquis communataire*.[29] This right covers audio-visual material as well as sound performances. The rationale for this exclusive right would seem to be the heightened danger of piracy in the electronic marketplace.

Article 3(3) provides that the consent of a right-holder to online transmission of a work does not exhaust his rights over the work. This applies to both the communication to the public right and the making available right. Whilst these rights exist, they can be exercised an unlimited number of times. Article 3(3) is a restatement of existing law, as set out by the Court[30] and the Rental Rights Directive.[31]

5.2.2 Distribution right

The Draft Directive provides in Article 4(1) for authors to have the exclusive right of authorising distribution of the "original of their works and copies thereof", in line with Article 6(1) WCT. The expressions "original" and "copies" restrict the scope of Article 4(1) to tangible objects.[32] The second part of Article 4 harmonises the principal exception to the distribution right, namely exhaustion. It corresponds with Article 3(2) in providing that the right of distribution shall only be exhausted by a transfer of ownership by the right-holder or with his consent. This provision is designed to prevent any new barrier arising to the Treaty principle of free movement of goods.[33]

5.2.3 Exceptions to the restricted acts in Articles 2 and 3

Article 5 provides for limitations to the rights of reproduction and communication to the public (including the "making available" right). The limitations revolve around use of copyright material for research, teaching and other

[28] Per Proposal, n.16 above, at 34. An example of a near-on-demand service is where a particular film is broadcast every half-hour.

[29] i.e. Community law. See further, Proposal, n. 16 above, at 34.

[30] *Coditel v Cine-Vog Films* Case 262/81 [1982] ECR 3381; *Warner Brothers and Metronome Video v Christansen* Case 156/86 [1988] ECR 2605.

[31] Article 1(4).

[32] Proposal, n. 16 above, at 35.

[33] Article 28 EC.

private, non-commercial purposes. The limitations are similar to those in Article 16 WPPT, Article 10 WCT and the Database and Computer Programs Directives cited above. The list of exceptions is exhaustive, in order to maximise the degree of harmonisation. The provisions are a compromise between providing incentives to authors to produce original work and facilitating the distribution of such work. In accordance with the principle of subsidiarity[34] the list is one of options for Member States to take up if they choose, it is not obligatory. Thus, Member States have some room to adapt the Directive in order to fit it into their existing legal and cultural traditions. However, the use of an exception is subject to the "three-step" test contained in Article 5(4):

(1)   it must be confined to specific cases;
(2)   it may not be interpreted so as to prejudice unreasonably the right-holders' legitimate interests;
(3)   it may not be interpreted so as to conflict with the normal exploitation of the protected subject matter.

The Draft Directive provides for the obligatory exclusion of temporary acts of reproduction which are an integral part of a technological process for the sole purpose of enabling use to be made of a work or other subject matter.[35] This is designed to ensure that operators are not prohibited from retrieving data immediately prior to transmission. Retrieval is not of economic significance, only the transmission (or sale) is. Without the exception, retrieval could be considered an independent act of reproduction.

Article 5(2)(a) allows for limitation to the exclusive right of reproduction, provided for in respect of reproductions on paper or any similar medium, effected by the use of any kind of photographic or other process having similar effects. The wording "similar medium" restricts the scope of this limitation to tangible copies, although the method of production is irrelevant.

Article 5(2)(b) provides for an exception to the reproduction right in relation to private use of audio and audio-visual material. Thus for example, under Article 5(2)(b) an individual will be able to make a back-up copy of a video or CD-ROM. This exception is optional for Member States and makes no distinction between analogue and digital copying. Member States may choose not to implement it in relation to digital works reproduced under licence (e.g. software), on the basis that the licence dispenses with any need for private copying. For example, if an individual buys a licence of software, then there is no need for copying, since if that copy should ever become unusable, the individual will be able to obtain another copy from the licensor. Whether Member States take up this optional exception will depend on advances made in technology, particularly whether it will be possible in the future for right-holders to use technical measures to prevent unauthorised digital copying.[36]

---

[34] Article 5 EC.
[35] Article 5(1).
[36] Work is being done to develop technology to prevent, or at least enable the tracing of,

Article 5(2)(c) allows Member States to exempt specific acts of reproduction carried out by establishments accessible to the public, as long as no direct or indirect economic or commercial advantage is thus gained.[37] Public galleries and libraries can thus be exempted from the general rules (although some payment may still be required). The wording, *"specific* acts of reproduction", excludes the applicability of this exception to the *general* electronic marketplace. For example if a server in a public library makes available copyright work to external users, a licence from the right-holder will be required. This is in line with Article 10 WCT and Article 16 WPPT.

Article 5(3) allows Member States to limit the rights of reproduction and communication to the public under Articles 2 and 3 respectively. The first limitation relates to reasonable non-commercial use for the purpose of teaching or research.[38] Use of this limitation may be made subject to payment. Thus, for example, educational institutions will be able to post right-holders' materials on a website for students to access, and may be allowed to levy a charge to cover costs. Four further possible limitations are listed in Articles 5(3)(b) to (e). These are taken from the Berne Convention and relate to the use of excerpts in reporting current events, quotations for purposes of criticism or review and use for purposes of public security or for the purposes of the proper performance of an administrative or judicial procedure.

5.2.4 Technological measures and rights-management information

The Draft Directive imposes on Member States an obligation to take steps to prevent the development of devices or services which are directed at circumventing technology designed to protect copyright.[39] This provision is also to be found in the WCT and WPPT.[40] All activity ancillary to the development of such devices or services is prohibited, including manufacture, distribution and facilitation. Only "effective" technological measures are prohibited. This implies that right-holders must demonstrate the effectiveness of a particular

unauthorised digital copying. "Watermarks" and "tattoos" are two such technologies. See further, Green Paper on copyright (COM(95) 382) at paras 49–50; and the follow-up Communication (COM(96) 586), <www.ispo.cec.be/infosoc/legreg/docs/com96586.html#23>, at chs 2–3; T. Vinje, "A Brave New World of Technical Protection Systems: Will There Still be Room for Copyright?", (1996) 18 *EIPR* 431.

[37] Similar to Article 1 of the Directive 92/100/EEC on rental rights.

[38] Article 5(3)(a). The source must be indicated. See also the corresponding Article 6(2)(b) of the Database Directive and Article 10 of the Berne Convention.

[39] Article 6. See also the Commission Green Paper, *Combating Piracy and Counterfeiting in the Internal Market* <http://europa.eu.int/comm/dg15/en/intprop/indprop/922.htm>.

[40] WCT Article 11: "contracting parties shall provide adequate legal protection and effective legal remedies against the circumvention of effective technological measures that are used by authors in connection with the exercise of their rights under this Treaty". See also Article 18 WPPT. The USA has strongly backed the introduction of such measures: proposals submitted to the Committee of Experts on a Possible Protocol to the Berne Convention, Sixth Session, Geneva, 1–9 February 1996, WIPO document CP/CEVII/1–INR/CE/VI/1.

technological measure before being able to take action against it. These provisions of the Draft Directive are complementary to the *Directive on the Legal Protection of Conditional Access Services*,[41] which aims at ensuring that there is only lawful access to services such as video-on-demand and online databases. These services will usually involve copyright material.

Article 7 of the Draft Directive provides that Member States must provide adequate legal measures to stop any person removing or altering electronic rights-management information or knowingly dealing with material which has had such rights-management information removed (see also Articles 19 WPPT and 12 WCT). This covers acts such as removing text attached to a web-page indicating that it is protected by copyright. Only electronic rights-management information is covered and the acts must be done "without authority". Such authority might come from the right-holder or the law. The scope of Article 7 is limited to acts which lead eventually to a breach of copyright. Thus, for example, an individual who removes "© A. Smith 1998" from an image retained on his (private) home computer purely for personal use would not be in breach of Article 7.

5.2.5 Sanctions and remedies

Article 8 imposes an obligation on Member States to ensure that appropriate remedies are in place to deal effectively with infringement. This is further to the general Community law duty of Member States to ensure the effectiveness of remedies.[42] Article 8(1) provides that sanctions shall be "effective, proportionate and dissuasive".[43] The use of the term "dissuasive" implies that criminal penalties may appropriately be employed. Article 8(2) is more specific than Article 8(1) and leaves less room for Member State discretion. It provides that right-holders whose interests are prejudiced by infringing activity must be able to bring an action for damages and/or apply for an injunction and, where appropriate, have the infringing material seized.[44]

5.2.6 Application over time

Article 9 provides that the Directive shall apply in respect of all works which are, by the implimentation date, protected by Member States' legislation or

---

[41] Discussed in section 5.3 below.

[42] See *Commission v Greece* Case 68/88 [1989] ECR 296; *Von Colson and Kamann v Land Nordrhein-Westfalen* Case 14/83 [1984] ECR 1891; Commission Communication, *The Role of Penalties in Implementing Community Legislation* (COM(95) 162).

[43] See also Part III of the WTO/TRIPS Agreement on Enforcement of Intellectual Property Rights.

[44] See corresponding Articles 45, 44 and 46 TRIPS Agreement.

[45] Article 11 (1) provides for an implementation due-date of 30 June 2000.

which "meet the criteria for protection under the provisions of the Directive".[45] Contracts concluded before the entry into force[46] of the Directive will be unaffected (Article 9(3)).

5.2.7 Amendments to prior Directives

Article 10 brings the Directives on rental right and term of protection[47] into line with the WPPT. Article 10(1)(b) amends Article 10(3) of the Rental Rights Directive so as to remove its applicability to reproduction rights, and thereby implements Articles 10 and 16 WPPT. Article 10(2) replaces Article 3(2) of the Term of Protection Directive in accordance with Article 17 WPPT. Article (1)(a) deletes Rental Rights Directive Article 7, which harmonised relevant reproduction rights, and replaces it with the "new harmonisation" of Article 2 of the Draft Directive.

5.3 CONDITIONAL ACCESS SERVICES

5.3.1 In general

One of the principal growth areas in electronic commerce is that of conditional access services, such as on-demand supply of music, information, and video. Pay-TV is already the principal market for films in the Community.[48] Digital technology has created new opportunities for specialised pay-broadcasting, particularly in radio.[49] The electronic share of the publishing market is forecast to range between 5 per cent and 15 per cent by the year 2005.[50] Growth is likely to accelerate if the currently exponential development of technology continues.

To deal with the legal issues raised by conditional access services, the Council of Europe in 1991 adopted its Recommendation on the legal protection of

---

[46] 20 days after the day of its publication in the Official Journal (Article 12).

[47] Directives 92/100 and 93/98.

[48] 34% of movie spending per consumer, as against 31% in the cinema: Commission, *Proposal for a European Parliament and Council Directive on the Legal Protection of Services based on, or consisting of, Conditional Access* (COM(97) 356) at 5.

[49] See the "Notification of a partnership agreement to set up and operate a digital pay-radio business for Europe (Music Choice in Europe)", OJ 1997 C70/7.

[50] Proposal, n. 60 below, at 8. In relation to online databases, see the Database Directive (Directive 96/9/EC, OJ 1996 L77/20), which creates a *sui generis* right to prevent unauthorised extraction from databases. The aim of the Database Directive is to encourage investment in advanced information storage and processing techniques and to nurture the development of an information market within the European Union (Recitals 12 and 39). Regarding international developments in this field, see <http://www.wipo.int/>. Member states of WIPO have indicated their views on the Directive and database protection in WIPO document, SCCR/1/INF/2, those of inter-governmental and non-governmental organisations: SCCR/1/INF/3 (30 June 1998), at <http://www.wipo.int/eng/meetings/1998/sccr_98/index.htm>.

encrypted television services,[51] which encouraged the use of both civil and criminal sanctions to combat piracy.[52] Two years later the Commission's *Strategic Programme for the Internal Market*[53] noted the need for regulation of conditional access services and in 1994 the Commission issued its Communication, *Europe's Way to the Information Society*,[54] which announced the preparation of a Green Paper on the legal protection of encrypted services. That Green Paper, "Legal Protection of Encrypted Services in the Internal Market",[55] proposed harmonisation of Member States' laws, and received firm support from the European Parliament.[56] Work towards a Draft Directive was announced in the Commission's Information Society Rolling Action Plan of 1996[57] and completed in July 1997.[58]

5.3.2 Directive on Conditional Access Services

The Directive on Conditional Access Services,[59] adopted in November 1998 with an implementation date of 28 May 2000, aims to provide a legal framework to protect conditional access services from unauthorised use. The Commission has identified the following adverse consequences as resulting from unauthorised use:

(1)   loss of subscription revenues for the service provider;
(2)   financial harm to the conditional access provider;
(3)   indirect financial harm to the content provider;
(4)   higher prices for the consumer (as the service provider claws back revenue lost through piracy);
(5)   less consumer choice.[60]

There are presently wide variations in Member States' laws on the protection of conditional access services. Some national laws only cover broadcasting services,[61] others do not cover satellite broadcasting or services broadcast from outside national territory.[62] The scope of the Directive is identified as covering

---

[51]   Recommendation R(91)14 of the Committee of Ministers.
[52]   Principles II.2, II.1.
[53]   COM(93) 632.
[54]   COM(94) 347.
[55]   COM(96) 76.
[56]   Resolution of 14 May 1997.
[57]   COM(96) 607.
[58]   COM(97) 356.
[59]   Directive 98/84/EC, OJ 1998 L320/54. See also: Commission, *Proposal for a European Parliament and Council Directive on the Legal Protection of Services based on, or consisting of, Conditional Access Services* ("Proposal on Conditional Access Services") (COM(97) 356); Council Common Position at OJ 1998 C262/34.
[60]   Proposal on Conditional Access Services n. 60 above, at 9 in summary.
[61]   I.e. they do not cover online services.
[62]   Proposal on Conditional Access Services, n. 60 above, at 10. See also Commission Green Paper, "The Legal Protection of Encrypted Services in the Internal Market" (COM(96) 76), at 25.

any of the following services when provided against remuneration and on a conditional access basis (Article 2(a)):

"—television broadcasting, as defined in point (a) of Article 1 of Directive 89/552/EC;
—radio broadcasting, meaning any transmission by wire or over the air, including that by satellite, of radio programmes intended for reception by the public;
—Information Society services within the meaning of Article 1(2) of Council Directive 98/34/EC of the European Parliament and of the Council of 22 June 1998 laying down a procedure for the provision of information in the field of technical standards and regulations and of rules on information society services".

The reference to "radio broadcasting" in the second indent above includes not only sound signals but "possibly also data signals within the same channel".[64] The definitions of radio and television broadcasting do not include on-demand services, which come within the scope of the third indent, "Information Society services".

The central provision of the Directive is Article 4:

"Member States shall prohibit on their territory all of the following activities:
(a) the manufacture, import, distribution, sale, rental or possession for commercial purposes of illicit devices;
(b) the installation, maintenance or replacement for commercial purposes of an illicit device;
(c) the use of commercial communications to promote illicit devices".

This list of prohibited activities is taken from Principle I of the Council of Europe Recommendation R(91)14 on the legal protection of encrypted television services, which distinguishes between possession for private purposes and possession for commercial purposes, providing that only the latter is unlawful. The Directive follows this aspect of the Recommendation and does not penalise personal possession of an illicit device, on the basis that individuals will often not know whether a particular device is illicit or not. Further, the Community law principle of proportionality[65] requires that Community action goes no further than is necessary to achieve its aim, and sanctioning commercial parties should be sufficient to prevent the use of illicit devices. The definition of "illicit device" revolves around the use to which the device is put. Article 1(e) provides, "*illicit device* means any equipment or software designed or adapted to give access to a protected service in an intelligible form without the authorisation of the service provider".

The Directive contains an "internal market" clause, which prohibits Member States from establishing or maintaining conflicting provisions (Article 3):

"1. Each Member State shall take the measures necessary to prohibit on its territory the activities listed in Article 4, and to provide for the sanctions and remedies laid down in Article 5.

---

[64] See Proposal on Conditional Access Services, n. 60 above, at 12.
[65] See generally G. de Búrca, "The Principle of Proportionality and its Application in EC Law", (1993) 13 *YBEL* 105.

2.   Without prejudice to paragraph 1, Member States may not, for reasons which fall within the field co-ordinated by this Directive:
(a)   restrict the provision of protected services, or associated services, which originate in another Member State; or
(b)   restrict the free movement of conditional access devices."

Article 3 aims at ensuring the free movement of conditional access services in accordance with Article 49 of the EC Treaty. Article 3(1) obliges Member States to put measures in place which will create a "level playing field" of regulation within the Community. Article 3(2) is an assertion by the Community of exclusive competence achieved through exhaustive regulation. The wording, "reasons falling within the field co-ordinated by this Directive", is concerned with reasons relating to the control of illicit access to conditional services. Thus, for example, a Member State will still be able to control decoding devices on the basis of national security, even if those controls have some impact on the market for conditional access services.

The Directive provides for a comprehensive regime of remedies (Article 5):

"1.   The sanctions shall be effective, dissuasive and proportionate to the potential impact of the infringing activity.
2.   Member States shall take the necessary measures to ensure that providers of protected services whose interests are affected by an infringing activity as specified in Article 4, carried out on their territory, have access to appropriate remedies, including bringing an action for damages and obtaining an injunction or other preventive measure, and where appropriate, applying for disposal outside commercial channels of illicit devices."[65]

Article 5 prevents Member States refusing jurisdiction over a dispute on the basis that the *locus* of the damage lies outside its territory. The fact that the infringing activity is carried out on its territory is sufficient to establish jurisdiction. Article 5 is prescriptive in identifying appropriate sanctions. In particular sanctions must be "deterrent", which hints at the use of criminal sanctions.[66] However, under the EC Treaty it is ultimately for the Member States to choose the form and method of implementation of all Directives.[67] The Proposal referred to the enforcement section of the TRIPS Agreement, which in contrast does explicitly identify penal provision as an appropriate deterrent to piracy of conditional access services. The civil remedies identified in Article 5(2) are the same as those in Articles 44 to 46 of the TRIPS Agreement.

---

[65] Provision for seizure is also made by Article 7 of Directive 91/250/EEC on the legal protection of computer programs.
[66] See the similar provision in Article 8(1) of the Draft Directive on copyright, discussed in section 5.2 above; also Commission, *Communication on the role of penalties in implementing Community legislation* (COM(95) 162).
[67] Article 249 EC.

6

Data Protection

6.1 INTRODUCTION

Electronic commerce carries with it the danger that individuals will lose control over their personal data. It is generally accepted that individuals have a right to control their personal data, a right which derives from the more general right to privacy, as enshrined in the European Convention on Human Rights.[1] However, this danger has to be set against the commercial freedom of traders to collect and use data which individuals make available to them. Whilst users themselves can take steps to protect their data,[2] there is little doubt that legislation has a role to play. Within the Community the search for the solution to the conflict between privacy and commercial freedom has centred on the transparency of, and consent to, the process and purpose of collecting personal data. This principle of transparency has a long tradition in other areas of Community law, including administrative law[3] and consumer law.[4] In the field of data protection, the practical application of the principle has resulted in the registration of data collectors and the granting of rights to "data subjects" to check and correct information held on them.

The first European steps towards regulating data protection were taken through the Council of Europe Convention 1981.[5] This provided the impetus to much national legislation on the protection of personal data.[6] In the early 1990s the European Community started to take over responsibility for data protection

---

[1] "Everyone has the right to respect for his private and family life, his home and his correspondence" (Article 8). Article 10 grants rights relating to free speech and the acquisition of information: "everyone has the right to freedom of expression. This shall include freedom to hold opinions and to receive and impart information and ideas without interference by public authorities and regardless of frontiers".

[2] For example through use of the Platform for Privacy Preferences devised by the World Wide Web Consortium, detailed in the Commission's Working Party Opinion 1/98, "Platform for Privacy Preferences and the Open Profiling Standard", 16 June 1998, available at DGXV's website, n. 10 below.

[3] D. Curtin, "Betwixt and Between: Democracy and Transparency in the Governance of the European Union", in J. Winter et al (eds), *Reforming the Treaty on European Union: The Legal Debate* (Deventer, Kluwer, 1996), 95.

[4] See for example, Directive 84/450 on misleading advertising and Directive 93/13 on unfair terms in consumer contracts, which attempt to ensure the transparency of advertising and consumer contracts respectively.

[5] Convention 108 for the Protection of Individuals with Regard to the Automatic Processing of Personal Data.

[6] For example the Data Protection Act 1984 in the United Kingdom, detailed, (but not reproduced), at <www.open.gov.uk/dpr/dprhome.htm>.

from the Council of Europe. The last data protection instrument of the Council of Europe appeared in 1991.[7] The Community had not been wholly inactive prior to this point, but it would seem that there was some tacit division of competence. As the Community matured through the Single European Act 1986 and the Treaty of Maastricht in 1992, it was natural that it should assume responsibility for legal protection of personal data from the purely inter-governmental Council of Europe. The competence of the Community to act in the field of data protection is clear. The EC Treaty provides that the Community can take such action as is necessary to ensure the smooth functioning of the single market.[8] Data processing is a commercial activity, as any other, and thus subject to regulation in the interests of the single market. Further, there is evidence that citizens are concerned about the trails of personal data they leave behind when they use information networks.[9] Through Community harmonisation, data subjects are assured of some minimum level of protection, sellers are better able to satisfy the compliance requirements of different countries and there are reduced opportunities for individual Member States to try and attract data processing business by offering a lax regulatory regime.

With these factors in mind, the Council and the Parliament adopted in 1995 the Directive on protection of personal data, discussed below.

6.2 DIRECTIVE ON DATA PROTECTION

Directive 95/46/EEC on the protection of physical persons as regards the processing of personal data and the free movement of data ("the Directive") was adopted on 24 October 1995.[10]

The core obligation of Member States is contained in Article 1: "Member States shall protect the fundamental rights and freedoms of natural persons, and in particular their right to privacy with respect to the processing of personal data". Article 3 brings within the scope of the Directive the "processing of personal data wholly or partly by automated means".

---

[7] Recommendation (91)10, protection of personal data used for payment and other related operations.

[8] Articles 100 and 100a.

[9] According to the survey, "Information Technology and Data Protection", *Eurobarometer* 46.1 (January 1997), two-thirds of consumers were concerned about this.

[10] OJ 1995 L281/31. Proposal at OJ 1990 C277/3, see also the Parliament's Legal Affairs Committee, *Community activities to be undertaken or continued with a view to safeguarding the rights of the individual in the face of developing technical progress in the field of automatic data processing* (PE 56.386/fin Doc 100/79). Due date for implementation was 24 October 1998. A detailed report has been produced for the Commission on the application of the Directive to online services, J. Reidenberg and P. Schwartz, "Data Protection Law and On-line Services: Regulatory Responses", available at <http://www.europa.eu.int/comm/dg15/en/media/dataprot>. Also an Internet Task Force, based in Directorate-General XV of the Commission, has been set up to deal with Internet-related data protection issues.

Processing itself is defined as, "any operation or set of operations which is performed upon personal data whether or not by automatic means, such as collection, recording, organisation, storage, adaptation or alteration, retrieval, consultation, use, disclosure by transmission, dissemination or otherwise making available, alignment or combination, blocking, erasure or destruction" (Article 2(b)).[11] This clearly includes data processed electronically. It also includes data part-processed manually, for example via the telephone.[12]

It is clear that the Directive does not cover "generic" data, i.e. that which cannot be linked to a particular individual. Article 2(a) limits the scope of the Directive to information relating to an identifiable natural person: "an identifiable natural person is one who can be identified directly or indirectly, in particular by reference to an identification number or to one or more factors specific to his physical, psychological, mental, economic, cultural or social identity". Thus data on how many people are buying a particular book from an Internet bookstore is not protected by the Directive, as no individual is identifiable from this data. The further application of the definition of an "identifiable person" to the electronic environment is problematic. Dynamic and unique Internet Protocol addresses are attached to individual Internet sessions. These can be linked to a specific subscriber using data held by the service provider. The identities of owners of permanent Internet Protocol addresses are generally publicly available. Further, websites may capture a wide range of information from visitors' computers including the clock time, an e-mail address, the names of files, and other sites visited, all or some of which might enable the identification of an individual.[13]

The Directive requires information to be supplied regarding the following (Article 19(1)):

(a) the name and address of the controller and of his representative, if any;
(b) the purpose or purposes of the processing;
(c) a description of the category or categories of data subject and of the data or categories of data relating to them;
(d) the recipients or categories of recipient to whom the data might be disclosed;
(e) proposed transfers of data to third countries.

It is not clear how these information provisions operate in practice. For example, how much detail must be given about the "purpose or purposes" of the processing referred to in paragraph (a)? Is it enough to state that the data will be processed for commercial reasons? How many categories of data must be

---

[11] Compare the United Kingdom Data Protection Act 1984: "amending, augmenting, deleting or re-arranging the data or extracting the information constituting the data and, in the case of personal data, means performing any of those operations by reference to the data subject" (s. 1(7)).

[12] The justification for covering manually processed data is given in Recital 27, "whereas the protection of individuals must apply as much to automatic processing of data as to manual processing; whereas the scope of this protection must not depend on the techniques used".

[13] See generally, Commission Working Party Recommendation 1/99, "Invisible and automatic processing of personal data on the Internet performed by software and hardware" (23 February 1999), available at DGXV's website, n. 10 above.

disclosed under (c)? What is the meaning of "recipients or categories of recipients" in paragraph (d)? Is it enough to state that data might be disclosed to those who have a commercial interest in it? Paragraph (d) also refers to recipients to whom data "might be disclosed". Does this encompass all possible recipients? Is the test of the controller's intention subjective or objective?

The Directive establishes five principles relating to "data quality". These are broad in nature and aim to cover as many situations as possible, including the disclosure of data to a third party. The principles (Article 6) provide that data should be:

> "(a) processed fairly and lawfully;
> (b) collected for specified, explicit and legitimate purposes and not further processed in a way incompatible with those purposes; . . .
> (c) adequate, relevant and not excessive in relation to the purposes for which it is collected and/or further processed;
> (d) accurate and where necessary, kept up to date; every reasonable step must be taken to ensure that data which are inaccurate or incomplete, having regard to the purposes for which they were collected or for which they are further processed, are erased or rectified;
> (e) kept in a form which permits identification of data subjects for no longer than is necessary for the purposes for which the data were collected or for which they are further processed. . ."

The principle within Article 6(b), that data be collected for "specified, explicit and legitimate purposes", encapsulates the "data subject consent" rationale of the Directive.[14] The United Kingdom case of *Innovations (Mail Order) Ltd v Data Protection Registrar*[15] illustrates the importance of the principle (common to UK and Community Law). In this case the plaintiff operated a mail order business and maintained a list of the names and addresses of customers. The plaintiff sold information from the list to third parties. Customers were not always warned of this possibility when orders were taken over the telephone, although notification did occur with subsequent acknowledgements of orders. The Tribunal held that there was a breach of the principle of subject consent contained within the Data Protection Act 1985, despite the fact that the data would not be sold on until thirty days after the acknowledgement was sent out.[16]

It can be seen from Article 6 above that data processors must obtain subject consent if they wish to pass data to third parties. Notification must occur prior to the transfer of data and be clear. The United Kingdom case of *Linguaphone Institute v Data Protection Registrar*[17] provides a possible illustration of what

---

[14] See in particular, Recital 30: "Whereas, in order to be lawful, the processing of personal data must . . . be carried out with the consent of the data subject".

[15] Case DA/92 31/49/1.

[16] The Tribunal was here stricter than the Council of Europe's Recommendation on the protection of personal data used for direct marketing (Recommendation 85/20).

[17] Case DA/94/49/1.

will *not* be enough to comply with the consent requirement. The plaintiff used a small opt-out box in the bottom corner of advertisements. The Tribunal stated that the box:

"appears in minute print at the bottom of the order form. In the Tribunal's view the position, size of print and wording of the opt-out box does not amount to a sufficient indication that the company intends or may wish to hold, use or disclose that personal data provided at the time of enquiry for the purpose of trading in personal data".[18]

There is no reason why the same principles should not apply to websites. It will not be enough to provide a small opt-out box in an inaccessible corner or a hyper-link to an "opt-out page". The Directive requires that data collected be "adequate, relevant and not excessive".[19] It might be considered "irrelevant and excessive", for example, for an Internet bookstore routinely to collect medical information from its customers. A further example of "excessive" data collection might be taken from the USA, where some websites ask children to fill in "questionnaires" concerning parental income.

The Directive provides that data held should be current and "kept in a form which permits identification of data subjects for no longer than is necessary for the purposes for which the data were collected or for which they are further processed" (Article 6(1)(e)). Any further processing must fulfil the following criteria (Article 7):

(a) the data subject has unambiguously given his consent; or
(b) processing is necessary for the performance of a contract to which the data subject is party or in order to take steps at the request of the data subject prior to entering into such a contract; or
(c) processing is necessary for compliance with a legal obligation to which the controller is subject; or
(d) processing is necessary in order to protect the vital interests of the data subject; or
(e) processing is necessary for the performance of a task carried out in the public interest or in the exercise of official authority vested in the controller or in a third party to whom the data are disclosed; or
(f) processing is necessary for the purposes of the legitimate interests pursued by the controller or by the third party or parties to whom the data are disclosed, except where such interests are overridden by the interests for fundamental rights and freedoms of the data subject which require protection under Article 1(1).

The meaning of "unambiguously given his consent" in Article 7(a) is unclear. Elsewhere in the Directive the term "explicit consent" is used.[20] The difference between these two might be that "explicit consent" requires an opt-in, whilst "unambiguously to give consent" can be satisfied by mere notification of the data subject.[21] In the United Kingdom, the Data Protection Registrar has given

---

[18] Indeed, the Directive appears to require more information than the United Kingdom Data Protection Act 1984, in as much as it requires notification of the data subject's right to access information held on him.

[19] Article 6(1)(c).

[20] For example, Article 8(2)(a).

[21] I. Lloyd, *Information Technology Law* (London, Butterworths, 1997) at 101.

the opinion that companies wishing to sell data to "third companies" should use an opt-in, rather than an opt-out, system.[22]

All "data controllers" must comply with the Directive: "the natural or legal person, public authority, agency or other body which alone or jointly with others determines the purposes and means of the processing of personal data".[23] Thus, for example, a small business which uses a contractor to operate a website selling its goods, yet itself keeps paper records on its customers, is a "controller" for the purposes of the Directive.[24]

There is a general prohibition on the processing of personal data relating to racial or ethnic origin, political opinions, religious or philosophical beliefs, trade-union membership, health, and sex life.[25] Public authorities come under a duty to fulfil data collection duties in accordance with the principle of proportionality. Data collected must be no more than is necessary for the authority to fulfil its public duty. An illustration of this principle can be found in the United Kingdom case of *Rhondda Borough Council v Data Protection Registrar*.[26] The plaintiff had a duty to collect information for the purposes of levying a tax under the Local Government Finance Act 1988. This tax applied generally to people over the age of eighteen. The Council requested the dates of birth of all local residents and the Tribunal found that this was going further than needed; all the Council needed to know was whether relevant persons were over eighteen.

Data processors must ensure that data sent to them is reasonably secure, and where the "processing" of data involves transmission of data over a network, "the controller must implement appropriate technical and organizational measures to protect personal data against accidental or unlawful destruction or accidental loss, alteration, unauthorised disclosure or access".[27] Most operators in the electronic marketplace already have such measures in place for reasons of commercial confidentiality. In terms of websites, sellers usually store customer details on secure servers behind "firewalls" to minimise the possibility of unauthorised access.

Individuals have the right to access and check the data held on them (Article 12):

"Member States shall guarantee every data subject the right to obtain from the controller:
(a) without excessive delay or expense:
    —confirmation as to whether or not data relating to him are being processed and information at least as to the purposes of the processing, the categories of data concerned, and the recipients or categories of recipients to whom the data are disclosed,

---

[22] *Thirteenth Report of the Data Protection Registrar*, at 26–28.
[23] Article 2(d).
[24] This is in line with the concept of "data users" under the Data Protection Act 1984.
[25] Article 8(1).
[26] Case DA/90 25/49/2.
[27] Article 17(1). There is apparently no direct remedy available to individuals in the event of their personal data being disclosed.

—communication to him in an intelligible form of the data undergoing processing and of available information as to their source,

—knowledge of the logic involved in any automatic processing of data concerning him at least in the case of the automated decisions referred to in Article 15(1);

(b) as appropriate the rectification, erasure or blocking of data the processing of which does not comply with the provisions of this Directive;

(c) notification to third parties to whom the data have been disclosed of any rectification, erasure or blocking carried out in compliance with (b), unless this proves impossible or involves a disproportionate effort.

The wording, "communicated in an intelligible form" in Article 12(a)(2), would seem to include giving access to the information via a website or sending it by e-mail. Presumably, the reference to "intelligible" information means "intelligible to the data subject". The information will by definition be intelligible to the data processor. Thus, data must not be sent in computer code, for example. Further, it would seem that the data must be sent in a language which the data subject can understand. This should not be any great burden on data processors as data will almost always be collected in a language the data subject understands.[28]

The meaning of "excessive expense" in Article 12(a) is unclear. In the United Kingdom, data processors are permitted to charge up to £10 (about 14 euro).[29] It is noteworthy that the Directive allows data processors to require the fee before any request for information is considered, so that a data subject might have to pay money only to be told that no data is held on him. There is no provision for the fee to be refunded if the result of the access is the amendment of incorrect information.

Member States may adopt legislative measures to restrict the scope of the obligations and rights[30] provided for by the Directive when such a restriction constitutes a necessary measure to safeguard the following (Article 13(1)):

(a) national security;

(b) defence;

(c) public security;

(d) the prevention, investigation, detection and prosecution of criminal offences, or of breaches of ethics for regulated professions;

(e) an important economic or financial interest of a Member State or of the European Union, including monetary, budgetary and taxation matters;

(f) a monitoring, inspection or regulatory function connected, even occasionally, with the exercise of official authority in cases referred to in (c), (d) and (e).

(g) the protection of the data subject or of the rights and freedoms of others.

It is clear from Article 13(1) that public authorities holding exempted data on a particular individual can tell him or her that they hold no such data. The

---

[28] The main exception to this is where someone other than the data subject enters the data.

[29] The Data Protection (Subject Access) (Fees) Regulations 1987, SI 1987/1507.

[30] Specifically, Articles 6(1), 10, 11(1), 12 and 21.

individual will have no recourse under Community law if faced with such a situation, although this will not always be the case under national law.[31]

The Directive (Article 4(1)) provides that national law is to be applied where:

"(a) the processing is carried out in the context of the activities of an establishment of the controller on the territory of the Member States; when the same controller is established on the territory of several Member States he must take the necessary measures to ensure that each of these establishments complies with the obligations laid down by the national law applicable;

(b) the controller is not established on the Member State's territory, but in a place where its national law applies by virtue of international public law;

(c) the controller is not established on Community territory and, for purposes of processing personal data makes use of equipment, automated or otherwise, situated on the territory of the said Member State, unless such equipment is used only for purposes of transit through the territory of the Community."

It is not clear how these principles apply to the electronic marketplace. In particular it is unclear what "establishment" means, although Recital 19 does provide that "establishment . . . implies the effective and real exercise of activity through stable arrangements". One study has indicated that national laws are on diverging paths in interpreting this provision.[32] From Article 4(1)(c) it seems clear that foreign processors will fall subject to the Directive as they will be using equipment situated within the Community to collect (i.e. "process") data.

The complications of the provisions on applicable law are mirrored in the obligation under Article 18 of controllers to register with national authorities. It is unclear at present whether foreign websites have an obligation to register with national authorities when they collect data originating within the Community and Member States have taken divergent approaches to this question.[33]

It is likely that there will be lacunae in regulation as authorities attempt to pass on responsibility for a particular case. There appears to be no simple solution to this problem. One possible solution might be the creation of a European "super-authority". However, the establishment of such an authority might conflict with the EC Treaty principle of subsidiarity.[34] Also, a super-authority might be perceived as distant from both data processors and, more particularly, data subjects. The problem of overlapping jurisdictions would seem to be an unavoidable consequence of regulating data in a global electronic environment. As the Council of Europe has stated:

"as the volume of transborder flow increases, the control possibilities diminish. It becomes much more difficult, for example, to identify the countries through which

---

[31] For example, in England any refusal to supply information would be subject to judicial review.
[32] Reidenberg and Schwartz, n. 10 above, at 127. As an example of a potential difficulty, they argue that "cookies" (permanent files on users' computers by website operators to record the users' browsing behaviour) could constitute "establishment".
[33] Reidenberg and Schwartz, n. 10 above, at 125.
[34] Article 5 EC.

data will transit before reaching the authorised recipient. Problems of data security and confidentiality are heightened when data are piped through communication lines which traverse countries where little or no attention is accorded to issues of data protection.

In brief, when advanced communication networks enable businessmen on foreign travels to access their enterprises' data bases via hand-held computers plugged into sockets available in airports and to down-load data instantaneously into their computers across vast distances, the issue of national regulation of transborder data flows becomes problematic indeed".[35]

6.2.1 TRANSFERS OF DATA TO THIRD COUNTRIES

The Directive permits transfers of data only to "safe" third countries:

"(1) The Member States shall provide that the transfer to a third country of data which are undergoing processing or which are intended for processing take place only if . . . the third country ensures an adequate level of protection.

(2) The adequacy of the level of protection afforded by a third country shall be assessed in the light of all the circumstances surrounding a data transfer operation or set of data transfer operations; particular consideration shall be given to the nature of the data, the purpose and duration of the proposed processing operation or operations, the country of origin and country of final destination, the rules of law both general and sectoral, in force in the third country in question and the professional rules and security measures which are complied with in that country" (Article 25).

It is unclear what is meant by an "adequate level" of protection.[36] The criteria given are vague. Not only are a country's "professional rules and security measures" to be considered, but also the level of compliance with those rules. As an example, one country which almost certainly does not meet the criteria of Article 25 at present is the USA.[37]

There are five exceptions to the prohibition of transfers to countries which do not adequately protect personal data (Article 26(1)):

(a) the data subject has given his consent unambiguously to the proposed transfer; or
(b) the transfer is necessary for the conclusion or performance of a contract concluded in the interest of the data subject between the controller and a third party; or

---

[35] Council of Europe, *New Technologies: A Challenge to Privacy Protection?* (1989), at para.6.9.

[36] See generally, Commission Working Party on the Protection of Individuals with regard to the Processing of Personal Data, "Transfers of personal data to third countries: Applying Articles 25 and 26 of the EU data protection directive", Working Document DG XV D/5025/98 (available at DGXV's website, above, note 10), adopted 24 July 1998.

[37] The Community and the USA have been negotiating for some time in an effort to facilitate data flows to the USA, see DGXV's website, above, note 10. There is no general statute on protection of personal data in the USA (although strangely there is the highly specific Video Privacy Protection Act 1988 18 U.S.C. §§ 2710–2711 (1994), this protects data relating to the videos an individual has hired). There are a number of Bills currently before Congress, see further, J. Kang, "Information Privacy in Cyberspace Transactions" (1998) 50 *Stanford Law Review* 1193.

(c) the transfer is necessary for the conclusion or performance of a contract concluded in the interest of the data subject between the controller and a third party; or

(d) the transfer is necessary in order to protect the vital interests of the data subject; or

(e) the transfer is made from a register which according to laws or regulations is intended to provide information to the public and which is open to consultation either by the public in general or by any person who can demonstrate legitimate interest to the extent that the conditions laid down in law for consultation are fulfilled in the particular case.

The practicality of the Directive's provisions on transfers to third countries, and indeed any attempted control of data transfers, can be questioned.[38] The Directive provides no remedy to the individual who is prejudiced by a breach of these provisions. Any *national* remedy will be retrospective rather than prospective. Individuals will generally not be able to prove any particular transfer took place and once data is transferred, the damage will typically have been done. It is also unlikely that Community public authorities will be able to take any effective action against third-country data processors to whom data is unlawfully transmitted by a controller within the Community. In line with the OECD Guidelines[39] and the Council of Europe Convention,[40] the focus of the Directive seems to be the facilitation, rather than the inhibition, of transborder data flows.

[38] See A. White, "Control of Transborder Data Flow: Reactions to the European Data Protection Directive", (1997) *5 IJLIT* 230.

[39] OECD Guidelines Concerning the Protection of Privacy and Transborder Flows of Personal Data (binding on the Member States of the European Community). See also the 1985 Declaration on Transborder Data Flows and the declaration from the Ottawa Conference on Electronic Commerce of October 1998, "Ministerial Declaration on the Protection of Privacy on Global Networks" (DSTI/ICCP/REG(98)10/REV2) available from <http://www.ottawaoecdconference.org/>.

[40] Note 5 above.

7

Commercial Communications

Communications from sellers to buyers are an integral part of the electronic marketplace. The Community and the Member States currently enjoy dual competence in the regulation of commercial communications. Every Member State has in place some kind of self-regulation of commercial communication,[1] which makes it a difficult area to harmonise. The impact and even the content of self-regulatory rules are often difficult to assess. The rules are liable to change rapidly. Further, self-regulation is a process which is implicitly informed by social, cultural and economic circumstances. It is not easily subjected to harmonisation within as diverse a grouping as the Community.

Regulation of commercial communications is also affected by the right of freedom of expression.[2] Although there is no formal expression of this right within the EC Treaty, its existence within the Community order has been recognised by the Court, drawing on the European Convention on Human Rights[3] and the principles common to Member States' legal traditions.[4]

This chapter will deal with Commission initiatives in the area, the relevant Treaty rules and the Directive on misleading advertising. It should also be noted that the Draft Directive on electronic commerce contains provisions relating to commercial communications and these are discussed in Chapter 3 above.

7.1 COMMISSION INITIATIVES

The Commission proposed a framework to deal with the problems of commercial communications in its 1996 Green Paper, "Commercial Communications in the Internal Market".[5] The scope of the Green Paper is, "all forms of communication

---

[1] Report of the European Parliament on Commercial Communications (A4–0219/97), <http://www.europarl.eu.int/dg1/a4/en/a4–97/a4–0219.htm>, (the "Epades Report") at B9.

[2] See generally, B. Apt, "On the Right to Freedom of Expression in the European Union" (1988) 4 *Columbia Journal of European Law* at 69.

[3] Article 10.

[4] See, e.g., *Oyowe and Traore v Commission* Case 100/88 [1989] ECR 4285; *Rutili v Minister of State for the Interior* Case 36/75 [1975] ECR 1219; J.H.H. Weiler and N. Lockhart, " 'Taking Rights Seriously': The European Court and its Fundamental Rights Jurisprudence" (1995) 32 *CMLRev*. 51. The right of freedom of expression is not so deeply rooted as in the USA, where it has been established in the Constitution for many years and has a long history of vigorous protection by the courts.

[5] Green Paper (COM(96) 192 final). See generally J. Mitchell, "Response to the Commission Green Paper: Commercial Communications in the Internal Market", (1997) 20 *JCP* 371; C. Miskin and A. Vahrenwald, "Commercial Communications in the Internal Market—At What Price?" (1996) 11 *EIPR* 621.

seeking to promote either products, services or the image of a company or organisation to final consumers and/or distributors".[6] This covers all forms of advertising, direct marketing, sponsorship, sales promotions and public relations, and encompasses both public and private organisations.[7] The Commission's Green Paper moved the Community focus away from specific forms of commercial communication to all information flowing from sellers to buyers and potential buyers, an all-inclusive approach driven by technology.[8] The introduction of common, broad definitions will facilitate the task of regulating electronic commerce, where the nature of commercial communications can be difficult to define.[9]

In its Green Paper the Commission stated that:

(a) cross-border commercial communications are becoming more common;
(b) divergence between the national regulatory frameworks could create barriers to the free movement of communications services, and to the provision of redress where the law is breached;
(c) the development of new services accentuates the risk of this divergence giving rise to barriers;
(d) the importance of the provision of information concerning commercial communications is growing.[10]

To date, Community regulation of commercial communications has been limited to misleading advertising and sector-specific regulation.[11] There is no generalised regulation of unfair advertising or marketing.[12] The Green Paper proposed streamlining and centralising control of commercial communications at Community level, via a uniform assessment methodology and the creation of an Expert Group to rule on cross-border problems.

[6] Compare the narrower definition of advertising in Directive 84/450/EEC on misleading advertising (OJ 1984 L250/17), "'advertising' means the making of a representation in any form in connection with a trade, business, craft or profession in order to promote the supply of goods or services, including immovable property, rights and obligations" (Article 2(1)).

[7] This regulatory attempt to merge forms of commercial communications reflects the increasingly diverse methods used to advertise goods and services to advertising-averse consumers, on which see P. Sepstrup, "The Electronic Dilemma of TV advertising", (1986) *European Journal of Communication* 383.

[8] See the Commission's Green Paper, "Convergence of the Telecommunications, Media and Information Technology Sectors, and the Implications for Regulation" (COM(97) 623).

[9] For example, games on the website of a toy manufacturer might be considered entertainment or advertising. Drawing a line between different forms of communications is of course not entirely new for the law. In the USA broadcasters must separate "infomercials" from regular programmes and in the United Kingdom advertisements in newspapers must be clearly recognisable as such.

[10] At 1.

[11] On misleading advertising see section 7.3 below. This book will not detail the sector-specific measures, but one example is the teleshopping provision within Directive 89/522/EC on television without frontiers (OJ 1989 L298/23).

[12] It has been asserted that this lack of legislation is attributable to United Kingdom opposition: L. Kramer, *EEC Consumer Law* (Brussels, Story Scientia, 1986) at 158-159. See also, U. Bernitz, "The Legal Concept of Unfairness and the Economic and Social Environment: Fair Trade, Market Law and the Consumer Interest", in E. Balate (ed.), *Unfair Advertising and Comparative Advertising* (Brussels, Story Scientia, 1986). Bernitz gives as examples of unregulated advertising: suggestive advertising, discriminatory advertising, advertising interfering with privacy, denigratory advertising and the giving of inadequate information in advertising (at 61 et seq).

The Green Paper recognised that in the Community's duty to regulate commercial communications there are conflicting roles and responsibilities. On the one hand, the Community has a duty to protect consumers[13] and national cultures.[14] On the other hand, it has a duty to facilitate the free movement of commercial communications within the internal market.[15] Whilst commercial communications flow easily across borders, it is often difficult for any party prejudiced by a communication to obtain redress across a national border. The Directive on injunctions[16] goes some way towards ameliorating consumers' problems of obtaining such redress, although the Directive only deals with the consumer field, and even there does not entirely eradicate the barriers to the "free movement" of justice within the Community. There is also a co-ordinating body for national public advertising regulators, the European Advertising Standards Alliance, but this lacks legal power and its record of intervention in the market is weak.[17]

In 1998 the Commission issued a Communication as a follow-up to the Green Paper, which detailed its favourable reception and ratified the bulk of its content.[18] The principal provisions of the Communication are a statement of intent to apply a "transparent assessment methodology" to commercial communications, and the setting up of a Commercial Communications Expert Group.

The transparent assessment methodology is detailed as involving two steps. The first step takes an analytical overview of the impacts of any national measure potentially restrictive of the free movement of commercial communications measure or any harmonisation measure proposed by the Commission. This involves assessment of potential impact upon consumers, any public interest rationale, any impact upon other public interests, and the measures' sensitivity to cultural and social differences. The second step is the legal assessment of the measure. This step asks whether the measure is proportional, and in the case of Community measures, also whether the measure is coherent with other Community measures.

The Communication provides for the establishment of a Commercial Communications Expert Group, consisting of two representatives appointed by each Member State and chaired by an official of the Commission.[19] It is to have

---

[13] Article 153 EC.

[14] Article 151 EC, "The Community shall contribute to the flowering of the cultures of the Member States, while respecting their national and regional diversity and at the same time bringing the common cultural heritage to the fore".

[15] Under Articles 28 and 49 EC, discussed in Section 7.2 below.

[16] See further Chapter 8 below.

[17] See Epades Report, n. 1 above, at B9. Its role is limited to transmitting complaints about commercial communications from the country of impact to the country of origin.

[18] Commission Communication, *The follow-up to the Green Paper on Commercial Communications in the Internal Market* (COM(98) 121). This was issued in tandem with the Draft Directive on electronic commerce, which makes certain provision for commercial communications, discussed in Chapter 3 above.

[19] Communication at 14. It is perhaps surprising that there is no provision for formal participation by the Parliament.

four functions: first, to facilitate the exchange of views between the Commission and the Member States; secondly, to help the Commission to identify solutions to problems in the field of cross-border commercial communications; thirdly, to provide data and facilitate information exchange on national measures; fourthly, to provide information for the work of committees established by secondary Community law in the field of cross-border commercial communications services.

The Communication (at 15) goes on to identify six priority areas for the Expert Group's consideration:

(1)   the protection of minors, in particular differing national regulations on sponsorship of educational programmes, on direct marketing, on television advertising, and on sponsorship of sports events;
(2)   differing national marketing laws in areas such as discounts, gifts and prize competitions;
(3)   sponsorship;
(4)   misleading advertising, particularly in relation to health claims;
(5)   redress;
(6)   the national application of the assessment methodology detailed above.

It remains to be seen how the framework provided by the Communication will work in practice. Its assessment methodology would seem to be an improvement on the current situation. As Parliament has pointed out,[20] the infringement procedure relating to state breaches of Community law on commercial communications (as other types of law) is slow, opaque and can be ineffective.[21]

7.2 TREATY RULES ON FREE MOVEMENT OF GOODS AND SERVICES

The EC Treaty rules on the free movement of goods and services impact upon electronic commercial communications in two ways. First, such communications are services, and thus fall within the scope of Article 49 of the Treaty which seeks to ensure the free movement of services within the Community.[22] Secondly, commercial communications are a *factor* of the free movement of whichever good or service they are promoting, and thus benefit from the protection of Article 28 (which seeks to ensure the free movement of goods) in the case of goods and Article 49 in the case of services.

In terms of Article 28, the Court held in the cases of *Mars*[23] and *Verlag*[24] that

---

[20]   Epades Report, n. 1 above, at 10.
[21]   This topic is discussed in more detail in the conclusion.
[22]   Article 49 (ex-59) provides "Within the framework of the provisions set out below, restrictions on freedom to provide services within the Community shall be prohibited". The Court ruled that the Article had direct effect in *Van Binsbergen v Bestuur van de Bedrijfsvereniging voor de Metallnijverheid* Case 33/74 [1974] ECR 1299.
[23]   *Verein gegen Unweses in Handel und Gewerbe Koln e. V. v GmbH* Case C-470/93 [1995] ECR 1923.
[24]   *Vereinigte Familiapress Zeitungsverlags- und Vertriebs GmbH v Heinrich Bauer Verlag* Case C-368/95 [1997] ECR I-3689.

where advertising is intrinsic to the free movement of goods, any relevant national restriction can be tested against that Article.[25] *Verlag* involved the advertising of a lottery *service* which was designed to promote *goods* (a newspaper); thus the relevant Treaty provision was Article 28. The Court held that if a national rule is non-discriminatory on its face, yet nevertheless does, or might, hinder the cross-border movement of goods, it can only be justified under the Article 30 exceptions or the list of mandatory requirements of public interest established within the *Cassis de Dijon* line of jurisprudence, namely ensuring the effectiveness of fiscal supervision, the protection of public health, the fairness of commercial transactions, consumer protection, and environmental protection.[26]

As regards Article 49, the case of *Bond van Adverteerders v Netherlands*[27] held that "advertising broadcast for payment by a television broadcaster established in one Member State for an advertiser established in another Member State constitutes provision of a service within the meaning of [Article 49] of the Treaty".[28] A further example of the operation of these rules is provided by the case of *De Agostini*.[29] In this case, the Swedish Consumer Ombudsman issued injunctions against the broadcasting of specific television advertisements for children's magazines, skin-care products and a detergent. The adverts were broadcast on Swedish and United Kingdom television channels. The Court ruled that Member States could only justify national measures which actually or potentially restricted the free movement of such services where the restriction was proportionate and necessary to achieve mandatory requirements of public interest, or one of the aims laid down by the then Article 56 (now 46). The case concerned the Television Without Frontiers Directive[30] and it should be noted that Internet broadcasts are not "broadcasts" within the meaning of that Directive.

7.3 DIRECTIVE ON MISLEADING ADVERTISING

The Directive on misleading advertising[31] is the Community's principal instrument of secondary legislation in the area of commercial communications. The purpose of the Directive is to protect consumers, businesses and the public against misleading advertising.[32] It prohibits any advertising which misleads, or

---

[25] See generally R. Greaves, "Advertising Restrictions and the Free Movement of Goods and Services", (1998) 23 *ELR* 305.

[26] *Rewe-Zentrale AG v Bundesmonopolverwaltung fur Branntwein* ("*Cassis de Dijon*") Case 120/78 [1979] ECR 649. The list of mandatory requirements is an open list.

[27] Case 352/85 [1988] ECR 2085.

[28] Ibid. at para. 48.

[29] *Konsumentenombudsmannen (KO) v De Agostini (Svenska) Forlag AB and TV-Shop i Sverige AB* Case C-34–36/95 [1998] 1 CMLR 32.

[30] Directive 89/522/EC, OJ 1989 L298/23 (as amended by Directive 97/36/EC, OJ 1997 L202).

[31] Directive 84/450/EEC, OJ 1984 L250/17 (as amended by Directive 97/55/EC on comparative advertising, OJ 1997 L290/18).

[32] Article 1.

is likely to mislead, its audience, and which is likely to harm a competitor as a result of its misleading nature.[33]

The Directive's definition of advertising certainly encompasses electronic advertising: "the making of a representation in any form in connection with a trade, business, craft or profession in order to promote the supply of goods or services, including immovable property, rights and obligations".[34] This covers virtually all forms of commercial communication, both individual and collective, in all economic sectors.[35] The definition of "misleading" is similarly wide, being, "any advertising which in any way, including its presentation, deceives or is likely to deceive the persons to whom it is addressed or whom it reaches and which, by reason of its deceptive nature, is likely to affect their economic behaviour or which, for those reasons, injures or is likely to injure a competitor".[36]

This definition catches advertising without any need for proof of anyone having been misled. It is enough if the advertising is "likely to mislead".[37] However, it is unclear who must be misled, or likely to be misled. Is he the "average" consumer? Or does he encompass the full spectrum of consumers? The Court has taken as its starting point the average consumer,[38] although not all national courts have adopted the Court's approach.[39] The Directive provides that advertisers can be required by courts and administrative authorities to provide evidence to support factual claims made in advertising.[40]

It is questionable whether the Directive covers advertising which is disguised as information provision. It must be likely "to affect [consumers'] economic behaviour or . . . to injure a competitor". It would seem that these criteria are

---

[33] Articles 1 and 2. It should be noted that the original Proposal for a Directive was considerably wider than the final version, see L. Freedman, "Proposed EEC Directive on Misleading and Unfair Advertising" in G. Woodroffe (ed.), *Consumer Law in the EEC* (London, Sweet & Maxwell, 1984), at ch. 3.

[34] Article 2(1).

[35] Compare the exclusions contained in other Directives, e.g. of financial services in the Directive on distance contracts (Article 3(1)), discussed in Chapter 9 below, and of core terms in insurance contracts in the Directive on unfair terms in consumer contracts (Recital 19 and Article 4(2)), discussed in Chapter 8 below.

[36] Article 2(2). As regards "likely to affect the economic behaviour", Hoffman J. indicated in the English case of *Director-General of Fair Trading v Tobyward Ltd*. [1989] 2 All ER 266, that this simply meant that consumers would buy the product (relating to an identical provision in the national implementing legislation, the Control of Misleading Advertising Regulations 1988, SI 1988/915), at 270e.

[37] Article 2(2). Although the Court in *Complaint against X* ("*Nissan*") Case C-373/90 [1992] ECR I-131 insisted that actual misleading must have occurred, this decision has been convincingly criticised as running contrary to the meaning of the Directive (G. Howells and T. Wilhelmsson, *EC Consumer Law* (Aldershot, Dartmouth, 1997) at 139) and must be considered to have been wrongly decided.

[38] *Complaint against X* ("*Nissan*") Case C-373/90 [1992] ECR I-131.

[39] National courts are permitted to institute a higher level of protection than that provided for in the Directive under Article 7. In German law it is sufficient for 10–20% of consumers to be at risk of being misled: J. Möllering, "Das Recht des unlauteren Wettbewerbs in Europea: Eine neue Dimension", (1990) 36 *Wettbewerb in Recht und Praxis* 1 at 10, per G. Howells and T. Wilhelmsson, *EC Consumer Law* (Aldershot, Dartmouth, 1997) at 138.

[40] Article 6.

satisfied at least in the context of advertising directed at children which is disguised as information provision. The advertising "deceives or is likely to deceive", because children will generally not appreciate the commercial motive of the advertiser. The advertising is likely to affect their economic behaviour as they will buy, or pressure their parents to buy, the products in question. The threshold is likely to be higher in relation to advertising aimed at adults.

Choice between enforcement mechanisms is left to national law. The Directive provides that enforcement means shall include provisions under which persons or organisations, "regarded under national law as having a legitimate interest in prohibiting misleading advertising", can take legal action, including for an injunction, against misleading advertising.[41] Cross-border enforcement of the Directive is aided by its inclusion within the remit of the Directive on injunctions.[42] There is no provision in the Directive for the tying of advertising into any resulting contract, as there is in the Draft Directive on consumer guarantees.[43] Nor are Member States required to ensure that advertising which is found to be misleading is corrected, although the Directive does make a *recommendation* to this effect in Article 4(2). This is somewhat ineffectual as once a case has come before the relevant authority the advertising has usually run its course and an injunction to stop the advertising achieves little or nothing.

---

[41] Article 4(2).
[42] Discussed in Chapter 8.3 below (the Directive is due to be implemented in the Member States by the end of the year 2000).
[43] Article 2(2)(d), see further Chapter 8.2 below.

8

Consumer Protection and
Conflicts of Law

This chapter aims to deal with Community activity in the distinct but related fields of consumer protection and conflicts of law. Virtually all transactions concluded in the Community electronic marketplace fall within the scope of the major Community instruments which have been adopted in those fields. This chapter considers the Directives on unfair terms in consumer contracts, consumer guarantees, cross-border injunctions, and conventions on jurisdiction and applicable law.

8.1 DIRECTIVE ON UNFAIR TERMS IN CONSUMER CONTRACTS

The Directive on unfair terms in consumer contracts[1] was adopted in 1993. It is a "horizontal" measure, i.e. it is not limited to consumer contracts in specific economic sectors and there are few exclusions.[2] The vast majority of typical electronic contracts in the Community, such as buying a CD-ROM or information via a website, will fall to be regulated by the Directive.

The Directive defines "consumer" as follows: "any natural person who, in contracts covered by this Directive, is acting for purposes which are outside his trade, business or profession".[3] The precise meaning of "consumer" remains to be resolved by the courts. It is unclear, for example, whether a car mechanic who buys software to use in his garage is acting "outside his trade, business or profession", within the meaning of the Directive. Although the mechanic is just as much a contributor to the single market, and is as unlikely to read the applicable contract terms, as somebody buying software for home use, the decision of the Court in *The Republic v Di Pinto*[4] indicates that he is probably not a consumer within the meaning of the Directive.

---

[1] Directive 93/13/EEC (OJ 1993 L95/29). Proposals were adopted in 1990 (OJ 1990 C243/2) and 1992 (OJ 1992 C73/7).

[2] The principal exclusions relate to terms which reflect international conventions, and terms defining the main subject matter of the contract (see further below).

[3] Article 2(b).

[4] Case C-361/89 [1991] ECR I-1189, discussed in detail in Chapter 9.1 below. Compare English law, where such a person has been ruled a "consumer" under the Unfair Contract Terms Act 1977: *R & B Customs Brokers v United Dominions Trust Ltd* [1988] 1 All ER 847.

The core provision of the Directive is that unfair terms shall not bind consumers.[5] The Directive provides that a term is unfair if, "contrary to the requirement of good faith, it causes a significant imbalance in the parties' rights and obligations arising under the contract, to the detriment of the consumer".[6] Further guidelines on the nature of unfairness are given in Article 4, which refers to the nature of the goods or services, the other terms of the contract and the circumstances surrounding the conclusion of the contract. There is a list of seventeen indicatively unfair terms in Annex 1.[7]

The Directive is inapplicable to terms defining the main subject matter of the contract and the price, as long as these terms are in plain, intelligible language.[8] Article 5 requires all terms to be in plain, intelligible language and that where there is doubt about the meaning of a term, the interpretation most favourable to the consumer will prevail.[9] It is not clear what the attitude of the courts might be to Web-based sellers who have their standard terms in a language which is foreign to the consumer. Are those terms in "plain, intelligible language" within the meaning of the Directive? The Directive is partly based on a rationale of consumer welfarism,[10] and given this, it would seem that a foreign language could not generally be described as "plain, intelligible language". This interpretation places something of a burden on sellers to provide standard form contracts in a variety of languages, yet it can be argued that a seller who takes the benefit of selling to consumers abroad should also take this burden. Further, the seller can more easily have the terms translated than can a consumer, and sellers are always free not to sell to consumers who cannot understand the contract.[11] Much of the Directive is aimed at preventing unfair terms taking consumers by surprise and this danger is clearly present where a foreign language is used. Also, Annex 1(i) of the Directive lists as indicatively unfair those terms which have the object or effect of "irrevocably binding the consumer to terms with which he had no real opportunity of becoming acquainted before the conclusion of the contract".[12]

---

[5] Article 6.

[6] Article 3.

[7] As the list is merely indicative of terms which might be unfair it is known as a "greylist" (as opposed to a "blacklist"). Examples include terms which attempt to exclude liability for personal injury to the consumer and terms which attempt to limit the legal rights of the consumer in the event of inadequate performance by the seller or supplier (Annex 1 (a) and (b)).

[8] Article 4(2).

[9] This applies to consumer contracts the general Community law principle of transparency, the importance of which has been stressed by the Court in both commercial cases (e.g. *GB-Inno-BM v Confédération du commerce luxembourgeois* Case 362/88 [1990] ECR 683) and non-commercial cases (e.g. *Handels-OG Kontorfunktionaererernes Forbund i Danmark v Dansk Arbedjsgiverforening (acting for Danfoss)* Case 109/88 [1989] ECR 3199, on sex discrimination).

[10] See Recital 9 of the Preamble. The Directive has another rationale: the harmonisation of rules within the internal market in order to ensure a "level playing field" for sellers (Recitals 2 and 5).

[11] If any consumer should falsely claim that he understands the contract, he would later likely be estopped from claiming that this was not the case.

[12] As an example of the operation of this provision: the Finnish Consumer Ombudsman has decreed that video rental shops should give a copy of the terms to the consumer before the video is rented. These terms should not be in "small print" and should also be visibly displayed in the shop: *Consumer Protection* (Helsinki, Office of the Consumer Ombudsman, 4/95).

Thus it would seem that terms in a language foreign to the consumer are likely to be unfair *per se*. The seller will not be able to rely on them, even where they define the main subject matter of the contract.

Assessment of the fairness of a term involves consideration of the presence or absence of good faith on the part of the seller.[13] Recital 16 of the Preamble provides the following factors as particularly relevant to the assessment of good faith:

(a) the strength of the bargaining positions of the parties;
(b) whether the consumer had an inducement to agree to the term;
(c) whether the goods or services were supplied to the special order of the consumer;
(d) the extent to which the seller or supplier has dealt fairly and equitably with the consumer.

The first of the above criteria, the strength of the bargaining positions of the parties, is particularly relevant to the electronic marketplace, in which the seller will usually be in a stronger bargaining position than the buyer. Sellers will typically have high levels of both technical sophistication and economic power in relation to the average consumer. However, something other than the normal disparity in strength between a business and a consumer is targeted by Recital 16(a). A seller could not be said to breach this guideline merely by being in a stronger position than the consumer. The target of this provision would appear to be sellers who *abuse* a strong bargaining position, particularly when that position is *abnormally* strong.[14] Recital 9 reinforces this interpretation, stating that, "acquirers of goods and services should be protected against the abuse of power by the seller".

The second criteria of Recital 16, whether the consumer had an inducement to agree to the term, allows sellers a degree of flexibility in the price-term mix they offer consumers. For example, electronic sellers of software may wish to offer two different standard-form contracts, an "economy" contract with only limited liability, and a "full" contract with comprehensive liability. Given the consumer welfare rationale of the Directive identified above, sellers are likely only to be able to rely on this guideline as establishing good faith in circumstances where the consumer fully understands the inducement being offered. It will not be enough for the seller merely to claim that the cheapness of a service or product is of itself an inducement for a consumer to agree to an unfair term.

---

[13] Article 3. Although the wording of Article 3 (quoted above) might be taken as indicating that the absence of good faith is merely a typical feature of unfair contracts, the existence of guidelines to assess it indicates that it is an independent ingredient of unfairness. See generally, R. Brownsword, "Two Concepts of Good Faith", (1994) 7 *Journal of Contract Law* 197.

[14] Compare the concept of "abuse of a dominant position" in competition law (see Article 82 EC Treaty). An example of abuse of power might be a refusal to entertain consumer representations that a term is unfair. Parallels in contract law might be found in cases such as the (English) *Suisse Atlantique Societe d'Armament maritime SA v Rotterdamsche Kolen Centrale* [1967] 1 AC 361 where Lord Reid complained that the customer generally has no time to read contract terms, "and if he did read them he would probably not understand them, and if he did understand and object to any of them, he would generally be told he could take it or leave it", at 363.

The third factor in assessing the presence or absence of good faith under Recital 16 is whether the goods or services were supplied to the special order of the consumer. This affords protection to sellers who sell goods for which there is no market other than the consumer who ordered them, for example where a consumer designs and buys a T-shirt on a website.

The fourth criteria in Recital 16, the extent to which the seller or supplier has dealt fairly and equitably with the consumer, is the most wide-ranging: "the requirement of good faith *may be satisfied* by the seller or supplier where he deals fairly and equitably with the other party whose legitimate interests he has to take into account". Notice will be an important element in dealing fairly with the consumer. It might be thought that sellers could satisfy the requirement of good faith merely by giving "due notice" of what would otherwise be an unfair term. Given the consumer welfare rationale of the Directive identified above, this is unlikely to be the case and the more onerous a clause, the more notice the seller will have to give to satisfy the Directive's requirement of good faith. The United Kingdom's Director General of Fair Trading has stated: "The way in which terms are disclosed and explained to consumers is a key factor in assessing unfairness and good faith".[16] Within the Web environment, the minimum requirements to ensure the validity of any unusually onerous clause would seem to be simple language, in large typeface, presented to the consumer before the decision to buy is made. Whilst hyperlinked terms and conditions are likely to be valid in general, this is less likely to be the case for onerous terms.

Article 4(1) provides that the nature of the goods or services shall be taken into account in assessing the extent to which a term is fair. This seems to indicate that where goods or services are complex or alien to consumers, special care must be taken to ensure that consumers are not prejudiced by unfair terms in the relevant contracts. For example, a term in a software contract that any fault arising in the software must be proved by the consumer to have existed at the time of delivery would most likely be unfair, as the average consumer is not competent to prove such a thing.

Article 4(2) provides that, in assessing the unfair nature of a term, reference should be made, "as at the time of the conclusion of the contract, to all circumstances attending the conclusion of the contract and all other terms of the contract". Although Article 4(2) refers to the time of the conclusion of the contract, this does not necessarily exclude consideration of the potential effect of what, at the time of the conclusion of the contract, seems a harmless clause. To use the example of a software contract, a clause that defects should be reported within a week of delivery might seem harmless to consumers when they buy the soft-

---

[15] Recital 16, emphasis added.

[16] Office of Fair Trading, *Unfair Contract Terms* (May 1996) at 8. In the United Kingdom, notice has also been critical in determining the validity of exclusion clauses in commercial contracts, see e.g. *AEG v Logic Resource* (20 October 95) reported in (1995) 9 *Corporate Briefing* 22.

ware, but not so when they discover a defect a month later. Read in this way, Article 4(2) incorporates a degree of foresight.

The Directive is silent as to who has the burden of proving the unfairness or otherwise of a term, although the seller is at least likely to bear this burden in respect of any term falling within the indicative list of unfair terms; and given the consumer welfare rationale of the Directive, there is a strong case to be argued that the seller always bears this burden.[17]

The Directive excludes from its scope terms which are "approved" by legislation, regulation or international conventions:

> "The contractual terms which reflect mandatory statutory or regulatory provisions and the provisions or principles of international conventions to which the Member States or the Community are a party . . . shall not be subject to the provisions of this directive" (Article 1(2)).

Article 1(2) is designed to avoid clashes between divergent legal provisions. It implicitly acknowledges that terms which reflect mandatory statutory or regulatory provisions are unlikely to take consumers by surprise. Further, these terms have been subject to the political process and will therefore be likely to have had some consumer input. In the case of a cross-border transaction where the countries of the seller and the consumer have different mandatory rules, the conflict between them will be resolved by the applicable law.[18]

Under Article 7 of the Directive, it would appear that any electronic supplier may find his standard terms challenged by domestic or foreign consumer organisations:

> "1. Member States shall ensure that, in the interests of consumers and of competitors, adequate and effective means exist to prevent the continued use of unfair terms in contracts concluded with consumers by sellers and or suppliers.
>
> 2. The means referred to in paragraph 1 shall include provisions whereby persons or organisations, having a legitimate interest under national law in protecting consumers, may take action according to the national law concerned before the courts or before competent administrative bodies for a decision as to whether the contractual terms drawn up for general use are unfair".

The meaning of Article 7 was the subject of litigation in *R v Department of Trade and Industry, ex. parte Consumers' Association*.[19] The Consumers' Association alleged that the United Kingdom Government breached its duty to comply with Community law by implementing Article 7 via a provision which

---

[17] Contrast the view of the Department of Trade and Industry in the United Kingdom, "Unfair Terms in Consumer Contracts—Guidance Notes" (July 1995), at 14.

[18] See section 8.4 below.

[19] Case C-82/96 OJ 1996 C145/3. The question put to the Court was: "does Article 7(2) of Directive 93/13 impose obligations on Member States to ensure that national law, (1) states criteria to identify private persons or organisations having a legitimate interest in protecting consumers, and (2) allows such private persons or organisations to take action before the courts or before competent administrative bodies for a decision as to whether contractual terms drawn up for use are unfair?"

granted the right to go to court only to a government agency. The Consumers' Association argued that the Government should have granted rights to private consumer groups to take legal action against unfair terms. Before the European Court had the opportunity to pass judgment, the case was withdrawn[20] and the issue has become of secondary importance following the adoption of a Directive specifically designed to deal with the rights of consumer organisations to act across the Community on behalf of consumers.[21]

The provisions of the Directive on Unfair Terms are mandatory:

> "Member States shall take the necessary measures to ensure that the consumer does not lose the protection granted by this Directive by virtue of the choice of the law of a non-Member country as the law applicable to the contract if the latter has a close connection with the territory of the Member States" (Article 6(2)).

In the context of electronic commerce, Article 6(2) gives rise to the following question: if a consumer situated in the Community buys something from an Internet bookshop shop situated in the USA, does the contract have a "close connection" with the territory of the Member States? It would seem that the answer must be yes, as the place from which one party contracts would seem to establish a "close connection" with that place. This gives the Directive a global impact and requires sellers all over the world to take cognisance of it. Sellers wishing to avoid the application of the Directive to the contracts they make are of course free to refuse to contract with consumers situated in the Community.

8.2   DIRECTIVE ON CONSUMER GUARANTEES

Whenever consumers buy goods in the Community electronic marketplace they have certain rights, currently derived from national law, in respect of the quality of those goods. The Commission began the process of harmonising these national laws in 1996 by adopting the Draft Directive on consumer guarantees,[22] on which the Council and the Parliament reached agreement in May 1999.[23] The rationales of the Directive are firstly to harmonise national laws in order to provide a level playing-field for sellers and secondly to stimulate cross-border purchases by giving consumers confidence in a minimum level of rights.[24]

The Directive is a sister measure to the Directive on unfair terms in consumer contracts, discussed above. Whereas the Directive on Unfair Terms regulates "small print", the Directive on guarantees regulates the "substance" of con-

---

[20] Further to a change in government and policy in the United Kingdom.

[21] The Directive on injunctions, discussed in section 8.3 below.

[22] OJ 1996 C307/8 and revised Proposal at OJ 1998 C148/12; see also the Council's Common Position, published on the 30 October 1998 (OJ 1998 C333/46); Commission's earlier Green Paper on guarantees for consumer goods and after-sales service (COM(93) 509).

[23] Conciliation Committee text PE-CONS 3604/99, adopted by the Parliament 5 May 1999, and the Council 18 May 1999.

[24] Recitals 2 and 4 of the Preamble to the Directive.

sumer contracts. The scope of the Directive is limited to consumer sales of movable goods.[25] Within the electronic marketplace the Directive thus principally concerns goods bought electronically and then physically shipped to the consumer. It does not apply to services which are delivered electronically. "Consumer" is defined as, "any natural person who . . . is acting for purposes which are not related to his trade, business or profession".[26] This is similar to the definition of "consumer" given in the Directive on unfair terms.[27]

One of the most striking features of the Directive from the vantage point of the electronic marketplace is that it will allow consumers to rely on *manufacturers'* advertising in order to claim against the *seller* that goods are not in "conformity with the contract".[28] For example, if a manufacturer of stereos has a website which advertises its stereos as having a certain level of power, a consumer buys the product and finds that this claim is false, the consumer will be able to claim against the seller for this lack of conformity. This type of claim fits neatly into the electronic marketplace, where consumers will often know which product they want and then choose the seller on the basis of price alone. Sellers are provided with certain safeguards regarding their potential liability for manufacturers' advertising. The consumer cannot rely on manufacturers' advertising where the seller:

—"shows that he was not, and could not reasonably have been, aware of the statement in question," (e.g. it was in another country)
—"shows that by the time of the conclusion of the contract the statement had been corrected, or
—shows that the decision to buy the consumer goods could not have been influenced by the statement." (E.g. it took place after the purchase).[29]

It is perhaps a marker for the future development of the law that the provisions of the Directive relating to "network liability" are a diluted version of the Commission's earlier Green Paper which suggested that the manufacturer be made *jointly liable* with the seller for goods not in conformity with the contract.[30] (The rationale of joint liability between manufacturer and seller

---

[25] Article 1(2)(b).

[26] Article 1(2)(a).

[27] A person "acting for purposes which are outside his trade, business or profession" (Article 2(b)).

[28] Article 2(2)(d) of the Draft Directive. Establishing a "network" of responsibility is not entirely novel for Community consumer law, see also the Package Holidays Directive 90/314/EEC, Article 3(2) of which states that "the particulars contained in the brochure are binding on the organiser or retailer".

[29] Article 2(4).

[30] Green Paper, at 86. In the United Kingdom a similar proposal was made by Law Commission Report *Sale and Supply of Goods* (Law Com No 160; Scot Law Com No 104, Cm 137, 1987). This Report was taken up by the ill-fated Consumer Guarantees Bill 1990 (a Private Member's Bill supported by the NCC). The DTI broached the issue again in its Consultation Paper *Consumer Guarantees* (February 1992). See further: H. Beale "Customers, Chains and Networks", in C. Willett (ed.) *Fairness in Contract* (London, Blackstones, 1997) at 137; C. Willett, *The Unacceptable Face of the Consumer Guarantees Bill*, (1991) 54 MLR 552.

being that modern consumers rely heavily on brand names when buying consumer durables in particular.[31]) The approach of the Directive is more limited than that of the Green Paper and is in line with current trends in national law, including that in the Netherlands[32] and Sweden.[33] Similar provision is made in New Zealand and proposed in the USA.[34]

Article 3 of the Directive provides that sellers will be liable for any lack of conformity with the contract that becomes manifest within two years of the sale. This is a limitation period rather than a period during which the consumer has any kind of absolute right to claim against the seller. For example, if a consumer buys a light bulb which fails after eighteen months' use, the consumer would not gain anything by the mere fact that this failure happened within two years of purchase.

The Directive provides that the reasonable expectations of the consumer will be a relevant factor in determining conformity with the contract.[35] Importantly, any lack of conformity becoming manifest within six months of delivery shall be presumed to have existed at the time of delivery unless this presumption is incompatible with the nature of the goods or the nature of the lack of conformity.[36] This presumption will be particularly important in technically complex goods where the non-expert consumer would find it difficult to prove that any defect existed at the time of sale.

In the case of lack of conformity, the consumer can demand any one of the following: recission of the contract, free repair of the goods, an appropriate price free reduction, or a replacement.[37] It might be thought that the choice between repair or replacement should lie with the seller rather than with the consumer, on the basis that otherwise the consumer might gain a windfall by having a (new) replacement after having used the original goods for some time. However, it seems appropriate that the choice between repair and replacement should lie with the consumer because, first, repair often fails to cure the defect, and secondly, discretion over remedies should not lie with the party in breach (here, the seller).

The Directive provides for the legal enforceability of manufacturers' guarantees and that these must be set out in plain, intelligible language.[38] Further, the

---

[31] Joint liability would also arguably increase efficiency as manufacturers are in the best position to remedy defects arising after the sale.

[32] BW 7:8.

[33] §203 of the Nordic Sale of Goods Act.

[34] See the New Zealand Consumer Guarantees Act 1993, ss.2, 14; the American reforms are those proposed to the Uniform Commercial Code, see further Beale, n. 30 above, at 154.

[35] Article 2(2)(d).

[36] Article 5(3). Currently, most Member States' laws place the burden of proving that the defect existed at the time of sale on the consumer, although the Netherlands and Denmark have recently been moving towards reversing this, so that the burden lies on the seller (Green Paper, Annex 1).

[37] Article 3(2).

[38] Article 6. In a number of Member States it is currently unclear whether manufacturers' guarantees are binding or not, compare for example the English cases: *Shanklin Pier Co v Detel Products Ltd* [1951] 2 KB 854 (guarantee not enforceable for lack of consideration); *Carlill v Carbolic Smoke Ball Company* [1893] 1 Q.B. 256, CA (guarantee was binding after collateral contract found).

guarantee must state that the consumers' statutory rights are unaffected by any additional guarantee.[39] There is no specific provision in the Directive for public enforcement of this (or any other) provision, unlike the Directive on unfair terms, which laid a clear obligation on Member States to ensure the existence of effective enforcement mechanisms.[40] In the absence of any enforcement provision, it is unclear how effective the provisions of the Directive relating to manufacturers' guarantees might be. However, Article 10 of the Directive provides for its inclusion within the Annex to the Directive on cross-border injunctions, discussed in section 8.3 below. Also, in line with general Community law, if a Member State were not to take steps to ensure its enforcement, an action for judicial review could be brought on the basis of breach of the obligation to ensure effective application of Community law.[41]

In line with most other consumer protection Directives, the provisions of the Directive are mandatory and provide a minimum floor of consumer rights on which Member States may build, within the boundaries of the Treaty.[42] The Directive provides that consumer, should not lose the protection of the Directive by the choice of law of a non-Member State as that applicable to the contract, where "the contract has a close connection with the territory of the Member States".[43] Article 11 provides for a transposition due-date of 1 January 2002.

8.3 DIRECTIVE ON CROSS-BORDER INJUNCTIONS

The borderless nature of the electronic marketplace creates problems in cases of dispute both between sellers and buyers and between regulators and sellers. Distance, differing legal rules and differing language can all raise barriers to cross-border dispute resolution. These problems are particularly apparent in the consumer field, as consumers are generally poorly-equipped to overcome them and the value of the dispute will rarely justify the time and expense needed to do so. Thus, serious distortions can appear within the marketplace, as deficient goods and services are supplied to consumers who have little effective recourse against the suppliers involved.

With these problems in mind, the Community in 1998 adopted the Directive on injunctions for the protection of consumers' interests.[44] This Directive has a

---

[39] Article 6(2).

[40] Article 7, discussed in section 8.1 above.

[41] Article 10 EC. However, see the criticisms of this enforcement mechanism outlined in the conclusion.

[42] Articles 7 and 8.

[43] Article 7(2). There is an identical provision in the Directive on unfair terms (Article 6(2)) and its meaning is discussed in section 8.2 above.

[44] Directive 98/27/EC of the European Parliament and of the Council of 19 May 1998 on injunctions for the protection of consumers' interests, OJ 1998 L166/51. The principal preparatory documents are the Green Paper, "Access of Consumers to Justice and the Settlement of Consumer Disputes in the Single Market" (COM(93) 576); Action Plan on consumer access to justice and the settlement of consumer disputes in the internal market (COM(96) 13); Commission Proposal for a

number of implications for electronic commerce. First, it is a novel inroad into Member States' procedural laws. Although the Community has produced a considerable body of substantive law, Member States have generally been left to determine for themselves the procedural law which governs vindication of relevant rights.[45] Community harmonisation of procedural law will reduce the legal barriers between Member States and should thus stimulate the Community's electronic marketplace.[46]

The second aspect of the Directive with significance for the electronic marketplace lies in the enforcement role it gives to non-governmental organisations. The Directive makes provision for consumer organisations to bring actions for injunctions against sellers who are breaching any one of a list of nine Directives concerning consumer law.[47] This aspect of the Directive makes law enforcement less dependent on national borders and thus brings the law closer to the practice of the borderless electronic marketplace.

The mechanism provided to facilitate this cross-border enforcement revolves around the mutual recognition between Member States of the ability of "qualified entities" to take action before courts and administrative bodies.[48] For example, under the Directive, a Swedish consumer organisation there competent to take legal action on behalf of consumers, is able to so act in all other Member States. This system will not be entirely new for Member States such as Belgium, Finland and Luxembourg, which all have systems of licensing consumer groups to litigate on behalf of individual or collective consumer interests.[49] However, it will represent a new step for Member States such as the United Kingdom and Ireland which have traditionally restricted the right to litigate in the general consumer interest to public bodies.[50] As the Preamble to the Directive states, the concept of "quali-

---

Directive on injunctions for the protection of consumers' interests, OJ 1996 C107/3 (COM(95) 712); Council Common Position at OJ 1997 C389/4.

[45] In accordance with Article 189 of the EC Treaty. See for example: *Rewe-Zentralfinanz eG and Rewe-Zentral AG Landwirtshaftskammer für das Saarland* Case 33/76 [1976] ECR 1989; *Rewe-Handelsgesellschaft Nord mbH v Hauptzollamt Kiel* Case 158/80 [1981] ECR 1805.

[46] See Recital 4 of the Directive.

[47] Annex. The list is an open one, as demonstrated by the Draft Directive on the distance marketing of financial services (discussed in Chapter 2 above) which provides for its addition to the list. See further on non-governmental enforcement: Commission Recommendation on the main principles applicable to bodies responsible for the out-of-court settlement of consumer disputes (OJ 1998 L115/31), which states that such bodies should be independent, transparent, adversarial, effective, adhere to the law and allow representation.

[48] Articles 3 and 4(1).

[49] See further: on Belgium—Article 98.4 of Les Pratiques du Commerce et L'Information et la Protection du Consommateur (14 July 1991); on Finland—R. Brownsword, G. Howells and T. Wilhelmsson, "The EC Unfair Contract Terms Directive and Welfarism", in R. Brownsword et al (eds.), *Welfarism in Contract Law* (Aldershot, Dartmouth, 1996), at 293; Luxembourg—Loi relative a la protection juridique du consommateur 25 August 1983, modified by Loi de 9 August 1993 (Mem 1993, 1181), Article 5.

[50] See further the discussion of United Kingdom implementation of Article 7 of the Directive on unfair terms, above.

fied entities" is a reflection of the wider Community law principle of mutual recognition.[51]

The Directive can be seen as a progression towards the "free movement of justice", in the same way as the Community has long worked towards the free movement of goods, services, capital and workers. In an internal market it is to be expected that a buyer with a grievance should be able to access the seller as easily as the seller is able to access the buyer. This is not currently the case within the Community's internal market. Whilst sellers generally enjoy guaranteed access to all the Member States (through Articles 28 and 49 of the EC Treaty), consumers in one Member State wishing to exercise their rights against a seller based in another Member State face tremendous legal obstacles. The Directive goes some way towards establishing equilibrium in the market and will give consumers more confidence in purchasing electronically within the Community.

The Directive appears to be part of a trend of increasing European involvement in national procedure. The European Court has become increasingly strict in its insistence that national procedural rules should not impede the internal market, as evidenced for example by *Data Delecta*[52] and *Factortame*.[53] In a number of recent cases the European Court has ruled that national procedure must not be allowed to prevent the effective enforcement of Community rights. One of the most important cases considering this issue is *Van Schijndel*,[54] in which the Court assessed whether certain Dutch rules of procedure hindered the exercise of Community rights. It was held that it is for each Member State to establish procedural rules to govern actions designed to vindicate Community rights, subject to two qualifications: first, that those procedural rules must not be less favourable than those governing similar actions of a domestic nature (the principle of non-discrimination) and secondly, that those rules did not make the exercise of Community rights "impossible or excessively difficult".[55] The Directive also fits with the current vogue of the private enforcement of Community rights.[56] Increased representative Community rights for

---

[51] See Recital 11. For examples of the legislative operation of this principle, see the Directives detailing criteria for the mutual recognition of professional qualifications (Directive 89/48/EEC, OJ 1989 L19/16) and banking licences (Directive 89/646/EEC, OJ 1989 L386/1); regarding case law see in the context of free movement of goods, *Rewe-Zentrale AG v Bundesmonopolverwaltung fur Branntwein* ("*Cassis de Dijon*") Case 120/78 [1979] ECR 649.

[52] *Data Delecta Aktiebolag and Another v MSL Dynamics Ltd.* Case C-43/95 [1996] ECR I-4661. The Court ruled that a United Kingdom requirement for foreign plaintiffs to provide security for costs was contrary to Community law. See further K. Uff, "Security for costs against European Community Plaintiffs", (1996) 15 *CJQ* 193.

[53] *R v Secretary of State for Transport, ex parte Factortame Ltd* ("*Factortame I*") Case C-213/89 [1990] ECR I-2433 (the Court held that the English prohibition of granting interim injunctions against the Crown was incompatible with Community law).

[54] *Van Schijndel and Van Veen v Stichting Pensioenfonds voor Fysiotherapeuten* Joined Cases C-430/93 and C-431/93 [1995] ECR I-4705.

[55] Ibid., para. 17.

[56] The most important articulation of the growing importance of the private enforcement of Community law came in *Francovich and Bonifaci v Italy* Cases C-6 and 9/90 [1991] ECR I-5357, in which Italy was held liable in damages to an individual for failing properly to implement a Directive.

non-governmental organisations might have knock-on effects at the national level. Certainly there are precedents for such "trickle-down" effects.[57]

8.4 CONFLICTS OF LAW

8.4.1 Jurisdiction over contracts

Jurisdiction over electronic contracts concluded by parties domiciled in the Community is generally determined by the Brussels Convention on Jurisdiction and the Enforcement of Judgments in Civil and Commercial Matters 1968.[58] There are a limited number of exclusions.[59]

The provisions of the Brussels Convention differ as between consumer and non-consumer contracts. In terms of non-consumer contracts, Article 2 provides that persons domiciled in a state party to the Convention can only be sued in the courts of that state, except where the contract contains a contrary jurisdiction clause (this will often be the case in online commercial contracts).[60] To give an example of the operation of Article 2: an Italian manufacturer contracts online with a French consulting firm, the Italian manufacturer is free to provide that the contract is to be governed by the Italian courts. If there is no relevant clause, the French firm could only be sued in France and the Italian manufacturer could only be sued in Italy. There are limited exceptions to this rule, including that the defendant may be sued in the place of performance of the obligation in question.[61]

In terms of consumer[62] contracts for goods or services, the consumer can only be sued in his domicile,[63] although he can choose to sue either there or in the seller's domicile.[64] The application of these provisions is dependent on the contract being "preceded by a specific invitation addressed to him or by advertis-

[57] For example the principles of proportionality and purposive interpretation, see further N. Emiliou, *The Principle of Proportionality in European Law: A Comparative Study* (London, Graham and Trotman, 1996), and J. Bell and G. Engle, *Statutory Interpretation* (London, Butterworths, 1995) at 193.

[58] OJ 1979 C59/1, in force in all the Member States. Essentially the same rules are in force in EFTA states through the Lugano Convention 1988. See generally on the Brussels Convention, C. Clarkson and J. Hill, *Clarkson and Hill: Jaffey on the Conflicts of Laws* (London, Butterworths, 1997).

[59] Including marriages, wills and bankruptcy, (Article 1). It is unclear whether licences are covered, which is important to electronic commerce as software and audio-visual material is commonly licensed rather than sold as a good or service.

[60] The defendant's domicile is the most important factor in determining jurisdiction under the Convention. The domicile of a company is where it has a "seat" (Article 53(1)), which can be a registered or other official address.

[61] Article 5(1).

[62] "Consumer" is defined as a person contracting "for a purpose which can be regarded as being outside his trade or profession" (Article 13); strictly interpreted in *Société Bertrand v Paul OH KG* Case 150/77 [1978] ECR 1431 (does not sinclude small traders acting outside their concrete trade).

[63] Articles 13.

[64] Article 14.

ing", and the consumer in his domicile taking "the steps necessary for the conclusion of the contract" (Article 13(3)). These conditions seem to be satisfied in the case of Web-based selling, if it is accepted that websites are "advertising".

8.4.2 Choice of law in contracts

The position regarding choice of law is more complicated that that of jurisdiction. The principal instrument governing contractual choice of law within the Community is the Rome Convention on the law applicable to contractual obligations of 1980.[65] The Convention distinguishes between contracts where there is a choice of law and those where there is not. These two situations will now be considered.

8.4.3 Express choice of law

Most electronic contracts will contain a choice of law clause given that businesses are usually careful to identify the legal implications of their contracts. The clause may be express or implied. No particular form of words is necessary, and the choice of law may be indicated by the circumstances of the case.[66] For example, it would be enough for the contract to make reference to a particular country's statutes.[67] As with jurisdiction, different rules are applicable to choice of law within consumer and non-consumer contracts.

In non-consumer contracts, suppliers are free to choose the applicable law, subject to national mandatory rules. For example, a Community subsidiary of an American multinational may choose the law of New York as that applicable to all its contracts, including those made with parties based in the Community. It is immaterial whether or not the other party is aware of the clause. Article 3(3) provides that where there is a choice of the law of one country, yet all the other relevant factors of the contract are linked to a different, single country, then the "mandatory rules" of the latter country apply. "Mandatory rules" are those rules from which there can be no contractual derogation. Examples include rules relating to exclusion of liability[68] and to sex discrimination.[69] However, Article 3(3) will rarely be applied to international electronic contracts as such contracts involve more than one country and therefore *all* the relevant factors will generally not be connected to any *one* country.

---

[65] OJ 1980 L266. The convention is in force in all the Member States. There are only a small number of excluded contracts, including those relating to trusts, land and family matters (Article 1(2)).

[66] Article 3(1).

[67] This is indicated by the Giuliano and Lagarde Report which is annexed to the Convention and its principal interpretive document, OJ 1980 C282/1, at comment to Article 3.

[68] For example, the Unfair Contract Terms Act 1977 in the United Kingdom.

[69] For example, the Sex Discrimination Act 1975 in the United Kingdom.

The Rome Convention is more restrictive in relation to consumer contracts[70] than it is in relation to commercial contracts. It provides that a choice of law may not deprive the consumer of the protection afforded by the mandatory rules of the country of his habitual residence:

> "if in that country the conclusion of the contract was preceded by a specific invitation addressed to him or by advertising, and he had taken in that country all the steps necessary on his part for the conclusion of the contract" (Article 5(2)).[71]

As noted above in relation to jurisdiction, it seems clear that a website is "advertising" and thus a firm based in one Member State which sells over the Internet to consumers in other Member States will not be able to override the mandatory consumer protection laws of those countries.

The Rome Convention contains safeguards to prevent suppliers finding themselves unknowingly bound by foreign law. The Giuliano and Lagarde Report gives the following example:

> "if . . . the German replies to an advertisement in American publications, even if they are sold in Germany, the [Article 5(2)] rule does not apply unless the advertisement appeared in special editions of the publication intended for European countries".[72]

Translating this example into an electronic context, a web-based seller can warn consumers that he does not wish to contract with consumers from particular countries. He may go further and ask consumers to indicate their country of residence, rejecting unwanted transactions (although it should be noted that within the Community, a company adopting such a policy may breach competition rules[73]). Should any consumer cite a false residence in order to conclude a contract with a reluctant supplier, it is likely that this would be taken at face value and he would later be unable to claim the protection of the mandatory rules of his true country of residence.

8.4.4 No choice of law clause

Situations in which there is no choice of law clause are most likely to occur in one-off transactions such as where a business or a consumer e-mails or phones

---

[70] See generally, R. Schu, "The applicable law to consumer contracts made over the Internet", 1997 5(2) *IJLIT* 192. He compares the more flexible rules of the USA: "the rights and duties of the parties with respect to an issue in contract are determined by the local law of the state which, with respect to that issue, has the most significant relationship to the transaction and the parties" (§188 Second Restatement); §1–105(1) UCC provides that the law of the forum should be applied where this is appropriate in the light of the circumstances of the transaction.

[71] This reliance on "habitual residence" differs from the concept of "domicile" contained in the Brussels Convention.

[72] OJ 1980 C282/1 at 24.

[73] Articles 81, 28 and 49 EC respectively. A likely scenario of breach is where a company has subsidiaries in Member States and will only sell to consumers via subsidiaries in the consumer's home country. See generally, V. Korah, *An Introductory Guide to EC Competition Law and Practice* (Oxford, Hart Publishing, 1997).

a supplier with whom they have not done business before. In these situations there will often be no opportunity for either party to incorporate their standard terms and conditions. Another example might be a Web-based seller of goods or services who decides that it is good marketing policy not to provide overly detailed terms and conditions.[74]

In the case where there is no choice of law clause in a *consumer* contract, Article 5(3) specifies that the applicable law is that of the country of the consumer's habitual residence. In *commercial* contracts, the general rule where there is no choice of law is to apply the law of the country with which the contract is most closely connected.[75] There is a presumption that the contract is most closely connected with the country where the person who effects the "characteristic performance" is located. The Giuliano and Lagarde Report defines "characteristic performance" as follows:

> "It is the performance for which the payment is due, i.e. depending on the type of contract, the delivery of goods, the granting of the right to make use of an item of property, the provision of a service . . . which usually constitutes the centre of gravity and the socio-economic function of the contractual transaction".[76]

Given this definition, it is clear that the person who effects the characteristic performance of a sales contract will usually be the seller. Once the characteristic performance of the contract is established, a separate test is provided by Article 4(2) to determine the applicable law:

> "it shall be presumed that the contract is most closely connected with the country where the party who is to effect the performance which is characteristic of the contract has, at the time of conclusion of the contract, his habitual residence, or in the case of a body incorporate or unincorporated, its central administration".

Where the party effecting the characteristic performance enters into the contract in the course of his trade or profession, then the applicable law will be that of the country where he has his principal place of business, except where the terms of the contract specify that the performance is to be effected through a place of business in a different country, in which case the law of that country will apply.[77] For example, if a Spanish manufacturer sets up a website in Spain where wholesalers can order goods and there is no choice of law clause in the contracts, the sending of the goods will be the characteristic performance. If the contract does not specify from where the goods will be sent, Spanish law will apply as this is where the manufacturer is based. If the contract does specify from where the goods will be sent, then the law of that country will apply, e.g. if the contract specifies that the goods will be sent from a French warehouse, French law will apply.

---

[74] There seems no reason to doubt the legal efficacy of the common practice of using a website icon to "link" to standard terms and conditions.

[75] Article 4(1).

[76] Above, note 68, at 20.

[77] Article 4(2).

In the context of electronic commerce it is necessary to consider whether a server (i.e. a computer) can constitute a "place of business" within the meaning of the Convention. This is important as the place of business of a supplier can determine the law applicable to the contract. It is common for servers to be located in places other than that of the business, for example a French firm may use a server in Switzerland because it is cheaper than using a French one and it may use a server in the USA because it is faster for its customers in that country. Some businesses may try and escape a particular jurisdiction by placing a server outside its reach. However, the content of the Giuliano and Lagarde Report seems to indicate that a server cannot be a "place of business" within the meaning of the Convention. It provides:

> "the law appropriate to the characteristic performance defines the connecting factor of the contract from the inside, and *not from the outside by elements unrelated to the essence of the obligation* such as the nationality of the contracting parties or the place where the contract was concluded".[78]

It would thus seem that a server's location is no more relevant to the application of the Convention than the fact that a contracting company happens to use a foreign telephone or postal service. The Convention focuses on the substance of transactions, as opposed to their form.

8.4.5 Jurisdiction over non-contractual disputes

Jurisdiction over non-contractual disputes is governed by the Brussels Convention on Jurisdiction and the Enforcement of Judgments in Civil and Commercial Matters 1968.[79] Such disputes may arise for example in relation to negligence or to breach of an intellectual property right. The first-order rules are similar to those which determine jurisdiction over contracts, discussed in section 8.4.1 above. The Convention does not apply to defendants domiciled outside the contracting states. There is a presumption that the appropriate jurisdiction is that of the defendants' domicile.[80] Article 5(3) provides for an additional factor of "the place of the harmful event":

> "A person domiciled in a contracting state, may in another contracting state, be sued:
> . . . in matters relating to tort, delict, or quasi-delict, in the courts of the place where the harmful event occurred".

The European Court has stated that "matters relating to tort, delict or quasi-delict" includes all actions seeking to establish the liability of a defendant which are not related to a "contract" within the meaning of Article 5(1).[81]

---

[78] OJ 1980 C282/1 at 20. Emphasis supplied.
[79] OJ 1990 C189/1, in force in all the Member States. Essentially the same rules apply to the EFTA countries through the Lugano Convention 1988.
[80] Article 2.
[81] *Kalfelis v Schroder, Munchmayer, Hengst & Co.* Case 189/87 [1988] ECR 5564 at 5585.

The place where the harmful event occurs and the place of the defendant's domicile may be different. The *Mines de Potasse*[82] case indicates that where the harmful event can be "located" in more than one place, the plaintiff can choose in which of those places to sue. *Mines de Potasse* involved a leakage of pollution into a river, and the harmful event could be viewed either as the leakage or as the damage which occurred downstream and in a different country. An electronic example of this type of incident might be a computer virus which is negligently allowed to spread from one computer to another. In such a case the plaintiff could choose the forum most favourable to him, whether in terms of practical convenience, or in terms of substantive law. This choice will not be open to those who suffer secondary damage.[83] For example, if a virus is spread by a German company to a French company and thereby causes the latter's insolvency, the creditors of the French company could sue only in the country of the defendant's domicile, i.e. Germany.

In cases of breach of copyright, the harmful event might be locatable in a great number of countries. For example, if John Dickie unlawfully loads someone else's book onto his website in the United Kingdom and it is accessed by people all over the Community, there will fifteen possible fora for action. In *Shevill*[84] the Court of Justice ruled that the courts of each contracting state where a defamatory statement was received and where the plaintiff suffered damage were limited to awarding compensation for the damage sustained within their own national borders. Thus, as Mrs Shevill was suing in an English court over a defamatory statement in a French newspaper, she could only recover compensation in respect of damage suffered in England. However, the Court stated that if action is taken against the publisher in the publisher's home contracting state, the court there can award compensation relating to damage suffered throughout all contracting states. It is likely that the Court would apply the same reasoning to breach of copyright claims. However, *Shevill* can be criticised in relation both to defamation and copyright claims. These claims originate in personal rights and it has been argued that the place of the damage is truly the domicile of person with the right.[85] On the other hand, this would expose defendants to the risk of expensive suit outside their own fora.

---

[82] *Handelskwekerij G J Bier BV v Mines de Potasse d'Aslace SA* [1978] QB 708.

[83] *Dumez France v Hessische Landesbank (Helaba)* Case C-220/88 [1990] ECR I-49.

[84] *Shevill and Others v Presse Alliance S.A.* Case 68/93 [1995] ECR 415.

[85] J. Ginsberg, "Private International Law Aspects of the Protection of Works and Objects of Related Rights Transmitted Through Digital Networks", WIPO Report GCPIC/2, 30 November 1998, available at <www.wipo.int>, at 18.

9

Directive on Distance Contracts

9.1 INTRODUCTION

The Directive on the protection of consumers in respect of distance contracts[1] ("the Directive") is one of the most important measures adopted so far by the Community in the field of electronic commerce. It provides consumers with rights to information and a cooling-off period when they make contracts other than face-to-face. The original Proposal of 1992[2] was farsighted in its anticipation of the electronic marketplace. The Directive is an approximating, rather than a unifying, measure,[3] and must be transposed by Member States by 4 June 2000.[4]

9.2 DEFINITIONS

9.2.1 "Consumer"

The Directive states

" 'consumer' means any natural person who, in contracts covered by this Directive, is acting for purposes which are outside his trade, business or profession" (Article 2(2)).

The meaning of "purposes which are outside his trade, business or profession" is not clear. It *may* cover the business person making purchases which are incidental to his or her business. However, the decision of the European Court in *Di Pinto*[5] indicates that, as regards Community law, such a person is probably *not* a consumer. In this case, Mr Di Pinto was appealing against a criminal conviction for contravening a French law on "doorstep contracts".[6] He sold advertising space to a trader who wanted to sell a business. Mr Di Pinto

---

[1] Directive 97/7/EC (OJ 1997 L144/1) reproduced in Appendix 1 below.

[2] Commission, *Proposal for a Council Directive on the protection of consumers in respect of contracts negotiated at a distance* (COM(92) 11), OJ 1992 C176/14. Note also the amended Proposal at OJ 1993 C308/18.

[3] Article 14. Compare the Draft Directives on the distance marketing of financial services, and electronic commerce, discussed in Chapters 2 and 3 above respectively, which aim at unified law.

[4] Article 15.

[5] *The Republic v Di Pinto* Case C-361/89 [1991] ECR I-1189.

[6] The French law in question implemented Directive 85/577/EEC on the protection of consumers in respect of contracts negotiated away from business premises, OJ 1985 L372/31.

travelled to the trader's premises to conclude the contract. The European Court agreed with Mr Di Pinto that the trader in question was not "acting for purposes . . . which can be regarded as outside his trade or profession".

Notwithstanding the wording of the Directive and the decision in *Di Pinto*, Member States are free to exceed the standards of protection contained within the Directive. Article 14 provides:

> "Member States may maintain or introduce more stringent provisions than those contained in the Directive in order to ensure a higher level of consumer protection".

Classifying as consumers those commercial purchasers buying "incidental" goods would fit with the rationale of the Directive as a measure for the consolidation of the internal market.[7] The Directive can be seen as an attempt to consolidate the internal market by giving non-expert consumers the confidence to buy across borders.

The rationale of protecting consumers in respect of distance contracts revolves around the fact that these purchases are often made "in the dark". As Recital 14 provides: "Whereas the consumer is not able to see the product or ascertain the nature of the service provided before concluding the contract". The goods or service may be of lower quality than the consumer expected; the seller may be disreputable, even fraudulent. A consumer who is supplied with low quality goods will typically be in a weak bargaining position *vis-à-vis* the seller. With these factors in mind, the definition of "consumer" might be taken to exclude only commercial purchasers who are buying goods in the direct course of their business, e.g. a fruit seller buying fruit or a car manufacturer buying car components.

The definition contained within the Directive can be contrasted with that of the recent Council Common Position on the Commission's *Proposal for a Directive on consumer guarantees*:[8] "any natural person . . . acting for purposes which are not related to his trade, business or profession".[9] The current draft revision of Article 2–102 of the USA's Uniform Commercial Code defines consumer as follows: " 'Consumer' means an individual who buys or contracts to buy goods that, at the time of contracting, are not intended by the individual to be used primarily for professional or commercial purposes".[10]

9.2.2 "Distance contract"

The Directive's definition of "distance contract" revolves around the "exclusive use" of distance communication:

---

[7] The legal base of the Directive is Article 100a (now 95) of the EC Treaty, which provides that the Community may take measures as is necessary for the development of the internal market.

[8] OJ 1996 C307/8.

[9] OJ 1998 C333/48, at Article 1(2)(a). [Adopted as a Directive in May 1999, see section 8.2 above].

[10] <http://www.law.upenn.edu/library/ulc/ucc2/597art2.htm>.

" 'distance contract' means any contract concerning goods or services concluded between a supplier and a consumer under a distance sales or service-provision scheme run by the supplier, who, for the purpose of the contract, makes exclusive use of one or more means of distance communication up to and including the moment at which the contract is concluded" (Article 2(1)).

It is unclear what is meant by "for the purpose of the contract, makes *exclusive use* of". Does this cover the situation where a supplier demonstrates a product to a consumer in person, but sells it via distance communication? In view of the consumer protection rationale of the Directive, the word "exclusive" is likely to be read restrictively. Thus, the supplier who demonstrates a product in person, but sells it at a distance, *would* be caught by the Directive. In this case, the supplier has exclusively used distance communication *for the purposes of the contract*. The fact that the supplier has had face-to-face contact with the consumer *for the purposes of selling* is incidental.

The meaning of "distance sales or service-provision *scheme*" in Article 2(1) is also unclear. If a seller advertises in a local paper and accepts telephone orders does he or she have a "scheme"? As with the meaning of "exclusive use", the consumer protection rationale of the Directive makes likely a broad reading of "scheme". Consumers will usually not be able to ascertain whether a "scheme" exists or not. The consequences for a consumer of a purchase falling outside the Directive could be serious, i.e. the consumer being in possession of poor quality goods and having few practical remedies. On the other hand, although not all sellers will be in a position to send to the consumer the information required by the Directive, the consequences for sellers of not complying with the Directive are not as serious: non-compliance simply extends the time-limits for the consumer to exercise his rights. Sellers who find the provisions of the Directive to be onerous can refuse to sell to consumers other than in person.

9.3 EXCLUSIONS

The Directive excludes contracts for financial services, including insurance, banking, pension and investment services[11] (although the Commission has recently adopted a Draft Directive on distance contracts for financial services).[12] This exclusion fits uneasily. The rationale for protecting consumers who buy "in the dark" applies to contracts for financial services as much as to any other contract. Indeed, it can be argued that consumers are especially in need of protection in this area, as financial services are often complex and expensive.

In principle it might be sustainable to argue that contracts for financial services are so specialised that sector-specific regulation is needed. However, any such argument is inapplicable to the Directive on distance contracts as it provides that in all cases where there is conflict between its own provisions and

[11] Article 3(1).
[12] See Chapter 2 above.

those of sector-specific regulation, the latter will prevail (Article 11(3)). Further, the financial services industry is certainly not immune from creating consumer problems, as demonstrated for example by the periodic collapse of banks. It would seem that the lobbying power of the financial services industry is the reason for this exclusion.[13]

9.4 MANDATORY NATURE

The rights granted to consumers under national law transposing the Directive cannot be waived by the consumer (Article 12(1)). Nor can those rights be excluded by the choice of law of a non-Member State where the contract has a close connection with the territory of one or more Member States.[14] It would thus seem clear that a US-based seller, for example, cannot avoid the Directive when selling to consumers based in Europe.

The Directive does not specify that the choice of law must be that of the Member State which has the closest connection with the contract, only that the choice of law must be that of a Member State. Thus, it would seem from the face of the Directive that an American seller could specify French law as applicable to its contracts with United Kingdom consumers and English law as applicable to its contracts with French consumers. However, such a practice would be rendered ineffective by the Rome Convention on the Law Applicable to Contractual Obligations, Article 5 of which broadly provides that in standard consumer contracts, the applicable law is that of the state in which the consumer has his habitual residence.[15]

9.5 PRIOR INFORMATION

The Directive requires the seller to inform the consumer of, *inter alia*, the identity of the seller, the main characteristics and inclusive price of the goods, and the consumer's right of withdrawal.[16] The information is required to be provided "in good time prior to the conclusion of the contract". The meaning of "in good time" is unclear, but seems to mean that the consumer must have time to consider the information before the conclusion of any contract. In particular, the seller must not send the information in such a way that it does not reach the consumer until after the contract is concluded (e.g. sending the information by post when the contract is made over the Web). The information is required to

---

[13] The industry also managed to obtain an exemption from Directive 85/577/EEC on doorstep sales (Article 3) and a part-exemption from Directive 93/13/EEC on unfair terms (Article 4(2) and Recital 19). This power is also exercised at national level; insurance contracts are excluded from the United Kingdom Unfair Contract Terms Act 1977.

[14] Article 12(2).

[15] OJ 1980 L266. See further section 8.4 above.

[16] Article 4.

be provided "with due regard . . . to the principles of good faith in commercial transactions" (Article 4(2)). The incorporation of the principles of good faith enables the Directive to respond to changing circumstances and take account of the individual characteristics of the relationship between a seller and a consumer.[17]

There is no sanction specified for breach of the provisions on the supply of pre-contract information. This stands in contrast to the provisions on confirmation of details *post*-contract: failure to send confirmation of details after the contract is concluded extends the period in which the consumer can withdraw (see further 9.6 below). The lack of any sanction against sellers for failure to provide prior information appears to create a monitoring role for the national enforcement agencies who are charged under Article 11 with ensuring the effectiveness of the Directive. This is particularly so given that not all mandatory prior information must be confirmed post-contract (in particular information regarding the cost of using the means of distance communication, where other than the basic rate, and any minimum duration of the contract).

The Directive does not stipulate who is to bear the burden of proof regarding the supply of prior information, although Article 11(3)(a) provides that Member States may place that burden on the supplier. Presumably Member States will place the burden on the supplier—it is difficult to envisage circumstances in which it would be reasonable to place it on the consumer. It would usually be difficult for a consumer, with no record of an Internet exchange for example, to prove that the seller did not supply accurate prior information. The choice that the Directive grants to Member States in this area reflects the Community law principle of national procedural autonomy.[18] Notwithstanding this principle, there is an over-arching obligation on Member States to ensure the effectiveness[19] of Community law and it can be argued that to achieve this, the burden of proving the supply of prior information lie with the supplier.

9.6 WRITTEN CONFIRMATION OF INFORMATION

Information provided to the consumer before the conclusion of a distance contract will often be non-durable, via the telephone or the Web for example. The Directive makes broad provision for the consumer to receive a copy of the contract in a durable form:

> "The consumer must receive written confirmation or confirmation in another durable medium available and accessible to him of the information referred to in Article 4(1)(a) to (f), in good time during the performance of the contract, and at the latest at the time of delivery" (Article 5).

---

[17] See generally, R. Brownsword, N. Hird and G. Howells (eds.), *Good Faith in Contract: Concept and Context* (Aldershot, Ashgate, 1999).

[18] See in particular *Humblett v Belgium* 6/60 [1960] ECR 559.

[19] Article 10 EC Treaty.

Article 5 clearly refers to the individual circumstances of the consumer: "written confirmation or confirmation in another durable medium available and accessible to him". Thus, a consumer without a video player, for example, must not be sent information contained on video cassette. There seems no reason why e-mail should not be a "durable medium" as it can be saved and printed. There is a sanction specified for the failure of a supplier to provide confirmation: the seven-day cooling-off period is extended to three months.[20]

One of the pieces of information which must be provided is that of the consumer's right of withdrawal (Article 5(1)). However, there is no stipulation that this information should be presented in a conspicuous manner, as there is with regard to certain information in the United Kingdom Consumer Credit Act 1974, for example.[21] Article 4(2) does provide that information must be provided in a "clear and comprehensible manner", but this is a general provision applying to all information. The right of withdrawal is perhaps the most important provision of the Directive. Its value will be diminished if consumers are not aware of their rights because notification is contained in the small print of contracts. Of course it might be argued that a harmonising measure such as the Directive on distant contracts can only establish the substance of consumers' rights and it is for national law to determine matters of form, but this seems to draw an artificial distinction between form and substance. Norway (as a member of the European Economic Area) has used transposing legislation to fill this gap in the Directive, providing that a special annulment form must be sent to consumers who enter into distance contracts.[22]

9.7   RIGHT OF WITHDRAWAL

The Directive provides for a "cooling-off period" of seven days (Article 6). In the case of goods, the seven-day period runs from receipt. In the case of services, it runs from the conclusion of the contract, or, if later, from the receipt by the consumer of the confirmatory details.

The right of withdrawal does not apply in respect of contracts:

"—for the provision of services if performance has begun, with the consumer's agreement, before the end of the seven working day period referred to in paragraph 1;
—for the supply of goods or services the price of which is dependent on fluctuations in the financial market which cannot be controlled by the supplier;

---

[20] Article 6. This prescriptive approach to sanctions is somewhat novel in Community consumer law. For example, the Directive on doorstep contracts left to national law the matter of sanctioning failure to inform of the right of withdrawal: Council Directive 85/577/EEC on contracts negotiated away from business premises, OJ 1985 L372/31.

[21] See s. 61.

[22] Consumer Contracts Annulment Form Order 1997 (2 May) [1997] *Norsk Lovitund* 858. (Member States are free to exceed the levels of consumer protection provided by the Directive under Article 14).

—for the supply of goods made to the consumer's specification or clearly personalized or which, by reason of their nature, cannot be returned or are liable to deteriorate or expire rapidly;

—for the supply of audio or video recordings or computer software which were unsealed by the consumer;

—for the supply of newspapers, periodicals and magazines;

—for gaming and lottery services" (Article 6(3)).

Thus, contracts for lottery tickets, perishable food and engraved items grant the consumer no right of withdrawal. The special characteristics of the above would seem to justify their exclusion from the scope of the Directive. The exception for "goods or services the price of which is dependent on fluctuations in the financial market which cannot be controlled by the supplier", is potentially wide. This exception will operate in markets which are highly volatile and in which the consumer could make a profit by judicious use of the right of withdrawal, e.g. the foreign currency market. In theory, Article 6(3) could be applied to a wide range of goods and services including holidays, heating oil and perhaps anything which originates in a country other than that of retail purchase. However, the consumer protection rationale of the Directive indicates that this exception will be read narrowly. Only if consumers might realistically withdraw from a contract because of a change in price will the right of withdrawal be lost. Also, if sellers can insure against relevant fluctuations in the price, they might be considered able to "control" them within the meaning of Article 6(3).

Similar provision to that of the Directive relating to withdrawal is already in place in the national law of many Member States. As early as 1992, Member States had gone some way towards recognising the importance of a right of withdrawal in distance contracts. At that time, the right could be found in relation to mail order sales in the law of seven Member States and was protected on a voluntary basis in the other five.[23]

The Directive makes no provision for the protection of advance payments. A right of withdrawal means little to a consumer who has paid the purchase price only to see the supplier default, whether through fraud or insolvency. For this reason, it can be expected that a number of Member States will make provision in their national law for the protection of advance payments. This is already the case in Portugal, where consumers cannot be required to make any payment in advance, whilst in the Netherlands it is illegal for sellers to demand more than 50 per cent of the purchase price in advance.[24] Other methods of protecting advance payments include first, provision for the separate holding of advance payments until the expiry of the cooling-off period and secondly, provision of a guarantee fund. In respect of guarantee funds, the Council felt that "the introduction of a guarantee scheme in case of supplier default is a broader issue of relevance to all of the supplier's obligations and should be dealt with as such",[25]

---

[23] Proposal, n. 2 above, Annex 1, Table 3.
[24] Ibid. at 9.
[25] [First] Council Common Position, OJ 1996 C264/52 at iv.

which indicates that specific Community provision in this area may be made in the future.

9.8 RESTRICTIONS ON THE USE OF DISTANCE COMMUNICATION

The Directive prohibits the use of fax machines and automatic calling machines[26] without the prior consent of the consumer (Article 10). This is because automatic calling machines have great capacity to irritate consumers, and receiving fax messages costs money. Such provision will no doubt be welcomed at least in Member States such as the United Kingdom, where the sending of unsolicited faxes is currently lawful. Member States must ensure that other forms of unsolicited distance communication are only used where there is not clear objection from the consumer (Article 10(2)). Thus "preference service" lists must be in place, although it is unclear how effective these will be in relation to the ephemeral medium of e-mail. Member States may subject unsolicited communications to more extensive regulation than does the Directive. In particular, "cold-calling" by telephone may be prohibited, as in Denmark and Luxembourg.[27]

9.9 ENFORCEMENT

Member States are free to decide which public, private or professional body or bodies are to have powers to police the Directive (Article 11):

> "1. Member States shall ensure that adequate and effective means exist to ensure compliance with this Directive in the interests of consumers.
>
> 2. The means referred to in paragraph 1 shall include provisions whereby one or more of the following bodies, as determined by national law, may take action under national law before the courts or before the competent administrative bodies to ensure that the national provisions for the implementation of this Directive are applied:
> (a) public bodies or their representatives
> (b) consumer organisations having a legitimate interest in protecting consumers
> (c) professional organizations having a legitimate interest in acting".

This situation of clear Member State choice stands in contrast to the Directive on unfair terms in consumer contracts,[28] Article 7 of which arguably created a direct enforcement role for both public and private consumer organisations.[29]

---

[26] I.e. machines which contain recordings of a human voice.

[27] Proposal, n. 2 above, at 8–9. In the United Kingdom, the Direct Marketing Association Code of Practice forbids the use of wholly automated messages without the prior written consent of the consumer (2nd edn., 1997), at 9.25(a).

[28] Directive 93/13 EEC, OJ 1993 L95/29, discussed in section 8.1 above.

[29] See *R v Secretary of State for Trade and Industry, ex parte No. 1 the Consumers' Association and No. 2 Which? Ltd* Case C-82/96 OJ 1996 C145/3 (the case was withdrawn before it came before the Court). See further J. Dickie, "Article 7 of the Unfair Terms in Consumer Contracts Directive",

The original *Proposal for a Directive on Distance Contracts* did envisage granting enforcement powers to private consumer organisations.[30] The putative value of this provision stemmed from a number of sources. Powers held by public bodies are frequently "checked" to minimise the possibility of arbitrary action, and this makes for slow procedures. Speed in dealing with rogue traders is critical in maintaining consumer confidence. The importance of rapid action is particularly important in the electronic marketplace, where technology allows large-scale frauds to be carried out quickly, without leaving any kind of audit trail. Government organisations are prone to "capture"[31] by the businesses with which they repeatedly negotiate—the relationship can become too comfortable. Private consumer groups might be expected by their very nature to be more responsive to consumer concerns than public bodies. The funding of public bodies can be precarious, and their effectiveness dependent on the political views of the government. Finally, consumers may be reluctant to approach a government body with their problem if they feel politically distant from the government of the day, or if it is the government itself against which they have a complaint.

In sum, it would have been beneficial for the Directive to have laid down a minimum enforcement standard which included enforcement powers for those organisations, private or public, domestic or foreign, with a legitimate interest in protecting consumers. The Directive goes some way towards regulating enforcement, and there seems no logical reason why it should have stopped where it did. Of course, judicial review may be available if the performance of a public body is sub-standard, but this is too indirect a remedy to constitute effective consumer redress.

On a more positive note, the Directive does provide a framework to tie different actors in the supply chain into the enforcement process. It places some responsibility for the content of information on those who transmit it: "Member States shall take the measures needed to ensure that suppliers and operators of means of communication, where they are able to do so, cease practices which do not comply with measures adopted pursuant to this Directive" (Article 11(3)(b)).

From the point of view of the individual being able to rely directly on the Directive, it is noteworthy that Article 12 provides, "the consumer may not waive rights conferred on him by the transposition of this directive into national law". Previous Directives on consumer law have provided that the consumer cannot waive the protection conferred by "the Directive", rather than the corresponding national law. This change in wording may simply be a rationalisation of language, in that consumers typically rely on transposing national laws rather than Directives. However, where a Directive is not transposed, or is inadequately transposed, then it can become important for the individual to be able

---

[1996] *Consumer Law Journal* 112; R. Brownsword and G. Howells, "The Unfair Terms in Consumer Contracts Directive—some unresolved questions", [1995] *JBL* 243.

[30] Proposal, n. 2 above, Article 13.

[31] R. Tur, "Litigation and the Consumer Interest", (1982) 2 *Legal Studies* 135.

to rely on it directly. Direct reliance has been possible since the Court developed the doctrine of "direct effect" in relation to Directives in the case of *Van Duyn v Home Office*.[32] It is unlikely that the Court would disapply this fundamental doctrine in the case of the Directive on distance contracts on the basis of the wording of Article 12. It is noteworthy that subsequent Directives and Draft Directives have not followed the example of the Directive on distance contracts.

9.10 TRANSPOSITION

The Directive gives Member States three years, until 4 June 2000, to transpose the Directive into national law (Article 15(1)), a period longer than that provided for by the Directives on unfair terms in consumer contracts and on general product safety: eighteen months and two years respectively.[33] The three-year period provided by the Directive on distance contracts may be an attempt to prevent a recurrence of the regular failure of Member States to transpose Directives within the time-limit. The three-year period provided is surprising in view of the fact that the Directive had a long gestation period. All affected parties will have been aware of the likelihood of legislation at least since the Proposal of 1992. Member State inefficiency rather than lack of time would seem the most likely explanation of failure to transpose legislation on time. In view of the importance of the Directive to the rapid development of the electronic marketplace it is likely that Member States will be watched carefully to ensure that they transpose it on time.

.

---

[32] Case 41/74 [1974] ECR 1337.
[33] Directive 93/13/EEC on unfair terms in consumer contracts, OJ 1993 L95/29, and Directive 92/59/EEC on general product safety, OJ 1992 L228/24.

10

Foci and Futures

Community electronic commerce law is evolving. It is a mixture of soft- and hard-law, and of established, pending and proposed law. The number of Draft Directives issued in this area in the last few years is astonishing for a legislative machinery which is usually slow.

Two foci can be identified within this law, namely the individual and the market. The focus on the individual is strong in consumer protection measures in particular. He is conceptualised as both passively vulnerable to the predations of sellers and as an active motor of Community market integration. These "welfarist" and "market" conceptions of the consumer can be found, for example, within the Directives, discussed in the chapters above, on unfair terms, distance contracts, and injunctions; and the draft directive on distance financial services. With an eye to both welfare and the market, all these instruments make provision for certain information to be provided to consumers.[1] The Directive on unfair terms provides a good example of the dual nature of the focus on the individual. Under this Directive, consumers are provided with protection against unfair contract terms both as an intrinsic good and to give them the confidence to buy in the Community's single market.[2]

However, this focus on the individual seems to be limited to Community measures adopted within the specific framework of consumer protection. The consumer protection measures can be contrasted with the Directive on data protection, the Draft Directive on electronic commerce and current rules on commercial communications. In these areas the focus is on liberalising the market and little account is taken of the particular characteristics and interests of individuals. In terms of data protection this focus results in individuals having minimal control over their personal data, in particular being virtually powerless

---

[1] See further, the chapters dealing specifically with those subjects. These provisions reflect Article 153 of the EC Treaty, which acknowledges consumers' right to information. See also *GB-INNO-BM v CCL* Case C-362/88 [1990] ECR I-667, although the Court linked this right to services provided for remuneration in *SPUC v Grogan* Case C-159/90 [1991] ECR I-4621. See generally on provision for consumer information (and fairness) in Community law, N. Reich, "A European Concept of Consumer Rights: Some Reflections on Rethinking Community Consumer Law", in J.S. Ziegel and S. Lerner (eds), *New Developments of International Commercial Law* (Oxford, Hart Publishing, 1998), at 443–448.

[2] Recital 9: "Acquirers of goods and services should be protected against the abuse of power by the seller or supplier, in particular against one-sided standard contracts and the unfair exclusion of essential rights in contracts". Recital 5: "Whereas, generally speaking, consumers do not know the rules of law which, in Member States other than their own, govern contracts for the sale of goods or services; whereas this lack of awareness may deter them from direct transactions for the purchase of goods or services in another Member State".

to stop transnational corporations transferring data outside the Community.[3] Similarly, the home country control principle within the Draft Directive on electronic commerce imposes geographical, political, cultural and linguistic distances between regulators and the individuals affected by the regulation which is greater than that which would exist if the "host" country was the controller. The same is true in the sphere of commercial communications, where the individual seems to be forgotten in the drive towards enabling sellers to communicate freely across all Member States. Little regard is had for the specifities of regional culture or the vulnerable situation of some consumers.[4]

The different foci of consumer protection measures and non-consumer protection measures considered in this book most likely reflects their different institutional sources. The consumer protection measures have their genesis in the Commission's Consumer Protection Directorate,[5] whereas the other measures have mostly originated in its Internal Market Directorate.[6] As their names imply, these two Directorates have different orientations and it would appear that this significantly influences the content of measures which they bring forward. There can be little doubt that the early stages of formulating measures are critical to their final content.[7] Whilst the formulation of legislation will always involve conflict between liberalisation and protectionism, the divergence of foci within Community law between consumer-protection measures and non-consumer-protection measures reduces its coherence. This incoherence is particularly serious in the context of Directives, which must be transposed into national law, as transposition creates the possibility of further garbling of the law,[8] although the Court has recently become increasingly strict in its insistence on clear and precise implementing measures.[9] A more coherent approach would give market actors greater confidence in the marketplace and enable courts across the Community more easily to give harmonious interpretations of the law. The Council has implicitly acknowledged this lack of co-ordination in its

---

[3] See Chapter 6 above.

[4] See, for example, the definition of "consumer" in *Complaint against X* (*"Nissan"*) Case C-373/90 [1992] ECR I-131 and the discussion thereof in Chapter 7 above, also the case of *De Agostini*, discussed in section 7.2 above.

[5] Directorate-General XXIV.

[6] Directorate-General XV.

[7] As a note on the Community's law-making process, individual Directorates-General will generally be responsible for producing a first draft of any Proposal for a Directive. This may gestate for some time before any other Directorate-General comes to know of its contents, or even its existence. See generally N. Nugent, *The Government and Politics of the European Union* (Basingstoke, Macmillan, 1994); M. Raworth, *The Legislative Process in the European Community* (Deventer, Kluwer, 1993).

[8] On the case of the United Kingdom, see for example S. Weatherill, "The Implementation and Repercussions of Consumer Protection Directives in Domestic Law", in W. Heusel, *New European Contract Law and Consumer Protection* (Trier, ERA, forthcoming).

[9] See, e.g. *Commission v Germany* Case C-96/95 [1997] ECR I-1653 in which the Court ruled that Member State implementation must "guarantee the full application of the directive in a sufficiently clear and precise manner so that, where the directive is intended to create rights for individuals, the persons concerned can ascertain the full extent of their rights", at 1654.

1998 Resolution on the consumer dimension of the information society.[10] In this Resolution, the Council invited the Commission to examine existing consumer-related legislation in the new circumstances of the Information Society and to take the necessary steps to ensure that consumer interests are given full consideration in *all* Information Society proposals.[11] The lack of co-ordination between consumer and non-consumer measures was also recognised by the Treaty of Amsterdam, which inserted a new Article 153(2) into the EC Treaty, providing that "consumer protection requirements shall be taken into account in defining and implementing other Community policies and activities". Comparison might be made with the USA, in which a more vigourous and coherent approach seems to have been taken to the consumer interest.[12]

The disjointed conceptualisation within Community electronic commerce law can be further argued to be reflected in, and perhaps even partly a result of, its structure. A great many instruments have been considered in this book and they are not easy to aggregate. The law is a labyrinth, clouding the rules for all market actors. A particularly opaque area is that of amended Directives, in which it is the practice of the Community not to produce official consolidated versions. This problem will become more acute as the body of Community legislation grows. It would seem that Community legislation has built up to such an extent that a Code, or a series of Codes, would aid its comprehensibility. The Parliament called for the elaboration of such as long ago as 1989.[13] Academics have been at work in this field for some time and it would seem appropriate for the Community now to follow that lead.[14] Indeed, the construction of a *framework* code for electronic commerce, to be developed as necessary by the courts, might be identified as the most appropriate way for the law to deal with the dynamic character of the electronic marketplace.[15] Certainly, such a framework might help to reduce current discrepancy between the timescales of development of Community legislation on the one hand and the electronic marketplace on the other. The average timescale of the Directives discussed in this book is approximately two or three years from Proposal to Directive and then a further two or three years for national implementation. It is a glacial process in comparison with the development of the electronic marketplace.

[10] OJ 1999 C23/1.
[11] At paras 1.1 and 1.2.
[12] See R. Starek, "Consumer Protection in the Age of Borderless Markets and the Information Revolution", <www.ftc.gov/speeches/starek/ausp.htm>; R. Starek and B. Rozell, "The Federal Trade Commission's Commitment to On-line Consumer Protection", (1997) 15 *John Marshall Journal of Computer and Information Law* 679–702.
[13] OJ 1989 C158/400.
[14] See e.g. the identification of common European contractual principles (rather than a code) in H. Beale and O. Lando, *Principles of European Contract Law* (Groningen, Martinus Nijhoff, 1995); also A. Hartkamp et al, *Towards a European Civil Code* (Nijmegen, Kluwer, 1998).
[15] See L. Lessig, "The Path of Cyberlaw", (1995) 104 *Yale Law Journal* 1743.

10.1 FUTURE DIRECTIONS

The scale and content of the law discussed in this book indicates that it will be the Community, rather than individual Member States, which will dominate law-making in Europe's electronic marketplace.[16] The borderless nature of the electronic marketplace means that Member States will have little claim to autonomous legislative competence in the area. The Community has traditionally taken an expansive view of the legislative competence granted by the enabling provisions within the EC Treaty.[17] The majority of instruments dealt with in this book are Directives, which, although requiring national implementing legislation, originate in the Community and have the European Court of Justice as the ultimate arbiter of their meaning.[18] The Court's vigorous defence of the supremacy of Community law will ensure the disapplication of inconsistent national law.[19] Further, while Directives do require national implementing legislation, a variety of legal mechanisms have been developed which circumvent the importance of this requirement, namely direct effect, indirect effect, and state liability.[20]

The Community has acted, or proposed action, in all fields pertinent to electronic commerce. What might be termed the "Communitarisation"[21] of law in this area is particularly evident in the 1998 Draft Directive on the distance marketing of consumer financial services, which aims at complete harmonisation of Member States' rules.[22] All previous Directives on consumer transactions have provided Member States with the option of going further in protecting con-

---

[16] See in a general part, J.H. Jans, "National legislative autonomy? The procedural constraints on European Law", (1998) 25 *Legal Issues of European Integration* 25.

[17] See for example Directive 85/577/EEC on doorstep selling, adopted under the then—Article 100 as internal market legislation—harmonisation of door-to-door sales rules can hardly be regarded as essential to the development of the single market.

[18] See generally, P.-C. Muller-Graff, "EC Directives as a Means of Private Law Unification", and W. van Gerven, "The ECJ Case-law as a Means of Unification of Private Law?", both in A. Hartkamp et al, *Towards a European Civil Code* (Nijmegen, Kluwer, 1998).

[19] See *Costa v ENEL* Case 6/64 [1964] ECR 585: "The integration into the laws of each Member State of provisions which derive from the Community, and more generally the terms and the spirit of the Treaty, make it impossible for the States as a corollary, to accord precedence to a unilateral and subsequent measure over a legal system accepted by them on a basis of reciprocity", at 593–594.

[20] These principles are discussed further below, with the exception of indirect effect which dictates national laws should be interpreted as far as possible in accordance with unimplemented Community law, see *Von Colson & Kamann v Land Nordrhein-Westfalen* Case 14/83 [1984] ECR 1891.

[21] Note the difference between Communitarisation and Europeanisation, the latter referring to cross-fertilisation occurring in areas of law which are outside the Community's competence, e.g. the European Convention on Human Rights, per W. Van Gerven "Bridging the gap between Community and National laws: Towards a Principle of Homogeneity in the Field of Legal Remedies?" (1995) 32 *CMLRev* 679 at 698.

[22] See Recital 7 in particular. See further on the Draft Directive, Chapter 2 above.

sumers, within the confines of the Treaty.[23] Similarly, the Draft Directive on electronic commerce, discussed in Chapter 3 above, excludes Member State activity in its "co-ordinated field".

In contrast, Communitarisation would seem to be progressing at a slow speed in the areas of tax and copyright in particular. These areas of law are closely linked to national culture. Another area in which it is unlikely that the Community will make significant progress in the immediate future is that of criminal law, which is of relevance to the electronic marketplace in as much as it can be used to deter fraud. Although the Treaty of Amsterdam 1998 strengthened the third pillar of the Union, that dealing with Police and Judicial Co-operation in Criminal Matters, the emphasis remains on co-operation rather than legal harmonisation. However, it should be noted that the Council of Europe, often a path-breaker for the Community in the past,[24] has been active in the area, having adopted in 1995 Recommendation R95/13 on the harmonisation of criminal procedural laws relating to information technology.[25]

It would seem, in accordance with the principle of subsidiarity,[26] that the borderless nature of the electronic marketplace identifies the Community as a more appropriate legislator than the Member States. This has been recognised by both the Commission and the Council:

Commission, Draft Directive on electronic commerce:[27]

"the adoption of this directive will not prevent the Member States from taking into account the various social, societal and cultural implications which are inherent in the advent of the Information Society nor hinder cultural, and notably audiovisual, policy measures, which the Member State might adopt, in conformity with Community law . . ." (Recital 22).

Council, Common Position on a Decision adopting a multiannual Community action plan on illegal and harmful content on global networks:[28]

"in conformity with the principle of subsidiarity as expressed in Article 3b [now 5] of the Treaty, the objectives of the proposed actions cannot be sufficiently achieved by

---

[23] Thus they are labelled as "minimum Directives". Article 8 of the Directive 93/13/EEC on unfair terms in consumer contracts provides a typical example: "Member States may adopt or retain the most stringent provisions compatible with the Treaty in the area covered by this Directive, to ensure a maximum degree of protection for the consumer".

[24] For example in human rights see *Nold v Commission* Case 4/73 [1974] ECR 491 and subsequent EC Treaty developments; also in data protection, discussed in Chapter 6 above.

[25] Council of Europe, Strasbourg, 1995. This covers issues such as search and seizure, technical surveillance, co-operation with investigating authorities, and cryptography. See further, I. Carr and K. Williams, "Council of Europe on the harmonisation of criminal procedural laws relating to information technology", [1998] *JBL* 468. The Commission has also promised action on the current divergence of national laws in their treatment of electronic evidence (COM(97) 157) at III-4.

[26] Article 5 EC Treaty. The ability of this principle to limit Community activity at all is questionable, see N. Emiliou, "Subsidiarity: An Effective Barrier Against the 'Enterprises of Ambition'?", in D. O'Keefe and P. Twomey (eds.), *Legal Issues of the Maastricht Treaty* (London, Chancery, 1994). Compare K. Lenaerts, "The principle of subsidiarity and the environment in the European Community: Keeping the balance of federalism", (1994) 17 *Fordham Int. Law Journal* 846.

[27] Discussed in Chapter 3 above.

[28] OJ 1998 C360/83.

the Member States owing to the transnational character of the issues at stake and can, therefore, by reason of the pan-European effects of the proposed action be better achieved by the Community" (Recital 21).

The expanding coverage of Community electronic commerce law is dependent upon effective enforcement of that law. As the Court has emphasised, access to justice is an essential part of the internal market.[29] It is questionable whether the Community currently has the enforcement mechanisms necessary to provide a firm legal framework for the electronic marketplace. The principal Community-level enforcement mechanism is Article 226 of the EC Treaty, which empowers the Commission to sue a Member State for failure to fulfil its Community obligations, in particular the obligation timeously to transpose Directives into national law.[30] The effectiveness of Article 226 is hampered by a number of factors.[31] First, the Commission does not have the resources to conduct over-arching reviews of Member State implementation and most enforcement action is initiated by complaints.[32] Secondly, it is time-consuming, particularly in comparison to the pace of change in the electronic marketplace. It takes the Commission between one and two years to reach the stage of issuing a reasoned opinion, and then another two or three years for any resulting case to come before the Court. Thirdly, the process is not transparent. Complainants have no right to access the correspondence between the Commission and the Member State. This lack of transparency makes the process susceptible to political interference. Fourthly, there is no right of appeal from the Commission's decision.

Despite these long-standing flaws, there appears to be no immediate prospect of reform to Article 226. However, the Draft Directive on electronic commerce does make separate provision for rapid executive action by the Commission against those who breach Community law.[33] Also, the problems with Community-level enforcement are ameliorated by relevant provision for private enforcement. The best legislative example of this is the Directive on injunctions, which grants enforcement powers over Community consumer law to a large number of private and public consumer organisations.[34] The Court has also played a part in expanding the importance of private enforcement, by developing the direct effect of Community law, and the doctrine of state liability for

---

[29] *Data Delecta & Forsburg v MSL Dynamics* Case C-43/95 [1996] ECR I-4661.

[30] Of the Directives discussed in this book a good example of non-implementation is the Directive on unfair terms in consumer contracts, which Spain has not implemented as of May 1999, four years after the deadline expired (this is before the Court of Justice, Case C-318/97).

[31] See generally R. Mastroianni, "The Enforcement Procedure under Article 169 of the EC Treaty and the powers of the European Commission: Quis Custodiet Custodes?" (1995) 1 *European Public Law* 535.

[32] See in the context of consumer law, the Commission's working paper on enforcement of European consumer legislation, <http://europa.eu.int/comm/dg24/policy/developments/enfo/enfo01_en.html>: "When the Commission receives sufficient information showing incorrect application of consumer Directives, it can open infringement proceedings against the Member State. This occurs on the basis of complaints", at 4.

[33] Article 19. See further Chapter 3 above.

[34] Discussed in Chapter 8 above.

breach. The principle of direct effect allows individuals to rely directly on rights derived from Community law before national courts.[35] In the context of the laws discussed in this book, the doctrine is of most importance in relation to Directives, which have for many years been capable of producing direct effect against the state,[36] although not against individuals.[37] However, there have recently been signs that the Court's hostility to the direct effect of Directives as between individuals is waning. For example, the Court in *CIA Security International SA v Signalson SA and Securitel SPRL*[38] held that a particular Directive could create direct effects as between individuals when the state is interposed in their relationship (so-called "triangular" relationships). The harshness of the denial of horizontal direct effect has also been mitigated by the Court's creation of the doctrine of state liability in Francovich.[39] However, the overall picture of Community electronic commerce law is that of a Community which has a great deal of power to make law but little corresponding power to ensure that this law is adequately and uniformly applied.

Part of the solution to the above problems relating to enforcement may be found in what seems to be a nascent trend in Community electronic commerce law, that of strict regulation of remedies for breach. The traditional orthodoxy of Community law has been that the area of remedies for breach of Community law is the province of the Member States.[40] Yet this dichotomy of responsibility seems illogical in the context of the borderless electronic marketplace. It is legitimately to be expected that not only the law, but also remedies for breach of that law, will be similar within a single marketplace.[41] Whilst there is an overarching Community law principle that Member States must institute effective remedies for breach of Community law,[42] this principle does not *per se* result in harmonisation

---

[35] *Van Gend en Loos v Nederlandse Administratie der Belastingen* Case 26/62 [1963] ECR I.

[36] Since the case of *Van Duyn v Home Office* Case 41/74 [1974] ECR 1337.

[37] *Marshall v Southampton & South-West Hampshire Area Health Authority (Teaching)* Case 152/84 [1986] ECR 723.

[38] Case C-194/94 [1996] ECR I-2201. The case involved Directive 83/189/EEC on the provision of information in the field of technical standards. The Court did not mention its previous contradictory rulings. Also *Criminal Proceedings Against Rafael Ruiz Bernaldéz* Case C-129/94 [1996] ECR I-1829; *Panagis Pafitis v Trapeza Kentrikis Ellados AE* Case C-441/93 [1996] ECR I-1347. See further K. Lackhoff and H. Nyssens, "Direct Effect of Directives in Triangular Situations", (1998) 23 *ELRev* 397; P. Craig and G. de Búrca, *EU Law* (Oxford, OUP, 1998) at 206–210.

[39] *Francovich and Bonifaci v Italy* Cases C-6 &9/90 [1991] ECR I-5357. The doctrine holds generally that where an individual suffers loss by reason of a serious state breach of Community law, then the state is liable to the individual for that loss.

[40] See, for example, *Rewe-Handelsgesellschaft Nord mbH v Hauptzollamt Kiel* Case 158/80 [1981] ECR 1805, where the Court held that the EC Treaty, "was not intended to create new remedies in the national courts to ensure the observance of Community law other than those already laid down by national law", at 44. Also, Commission Communication, *The role of penalties in implementing Community internal market legislation* (COM(95) 162).

[41] Thus the Latin maxim, *ubi jus ibi remedium* (where there is a right there is a remedy). See generally, W. Van Gerven, "Bridging the gap between Community and national laws: Towards a principle of homogeneity in the field of legal remedies?" (1995) *CMLRev* 679.

[42] The principle of "effectiveness": Member State must ensure "that infringements of Community law are penalised under conditions, both procedural and substantive, which are analogous to those applicable to infringements of national law of a similar nature and importance and

of national remedies. The law discussed in this book shows an increasing prescription of remedies, something which seems to be a general trend in Community law.[43] Examples include: the Directive on injunctions (see Chapter 8.3), which prescribes the cross-border availability of injunctions; the Directive on conditional access services (see Chapter 5.3.2), which indicates that criminal sanctions are appropriate for specific breaches of its provisions; the Directive on distance contracts (see Chapter 9), which prescribes the remedies for non-provision of prior information (contrast its sister measure, Directive 85/577/EEC on doorstep selling, which left the question of remedies to national law).

A further direction of the Community law of electronic commerce is a tendency towards "hard law", rather than "soft law".[44] Most of this book is concerned with the instrument of the Directive, which is a binding instrument. Where the adequacy of soft law has been tested, for example in the areas of distance contracts and cross-border credit transfers, it has been found wanting.[45] Whilst soft law might save public money because its public enforcement costs are low or non-existent, it only works effectively in markets where there are low compliance costs, cohesive groups of sellers, low costs of detection of breach and adequate sanctions.[46] In those types of market, suppliers tend to have long-established and valuable reputations. On the other hand, in diffuse markets, such as that of electronic commerce, there is little pressure on suppliers to comply with soft law. In particular, threats to eject a supplier from the electronic marketplace have little force as it will usually be easy for the supplier to re-establish with a different identity.

This move towards hard law can be found even within the Directives themselves. The Directive on distance contracts provides:

which, in any event, make the penalty effective, proportionate and dissuasive": *Commission v Greece* Case 68/88 [1989] ECR 2979 at 24. See also *R v Secretary of State for Transport, ex parte Factortame Ltd and others* Case C-213/89 [1990] ECR I-2433; *Dekker Stichting voor Jong Volwassenen (VJV) Plus* Case C-177/88 [1990] I-ECR 3941; *R v Secretary of State for Social Security, ex parte Eunice Sutton* Case C-66/95 [1997] ECR I-2163.

[43] See Commission Communication, *Towards a greater efficiency in obtention and enforcement of judgments in the European Community*, which focuses on the harmonisation of aspects of procedural law (COM(97) 609).

[44] "Hard law" meaning law which is binding, "soft law" meaning non-binding measures such as Recommendations aimed at encouraging action at a national level or developing voluntary self-regulatory standards. It should be noted however that soft law is not entirely without legal effect, it can be used as an interpretative aid: *Grimaldi v FNF* Case C-322/88 [1989] ECR 4407.

[45] Commission Recommendation 92/295 on distance contracts, OJ 1992 L156/21, has been replaced by Directive 97/7/EEC, discussed in Chapter 9 above. Commission Recommendation 90/109/EEC on the transparency of banking conditions relating to cross-border financial transactions, OJ 1990 L67/39 has now been replaced by Directive 97/5/EC on cross-border credit transfers, OJ 1997 L42/25. See further in relation to consumer soft law, G. Howells, "'Soft law' in EC consumer law", in P. Craig and C. Harlow (eds), *Law-making in the European Union* (Cambridge (MA), Kluwer, 1998).

[46] I. Ramsay, *Consumer Protection* (London, Weidenfeld & Nicolson, 1989) at 91. See in the specific context of consumer law, European Consumer Law Group, "Non-Legislative Means of Consumer Protection" (1983) 6 *Journal of Consumer Policy* 209.

"Member States may provide that voluntary supervision of compliance with the provisions of this Directive entrusted to self-regulatory bodies and recourse to such bodies to settle disputes are added to the means which Member States must provide to ensure compliance with the provisions of this Directive" (Article 11(4)).

This sends a clear message to countries which in the past have relied heavily on self-regulation, such as the United Kingdom,[47] that in the field of distance contracts, self-regulation will not of itself suffice.

10.2 A TRADITIONAL LEGAL FRAMEWORK FOR ELECTRONIC COMMERCE OR A "BRAVE NEW WORLD"?

The global electronic marketplace currently operates within a "traditional" legal framework, where "local" (including Community) laws are applied to actions which are carried out in, or impact within, a particular locality. Notwithstanding the specific case of the Community, little effort is made to co-ordinate or homogenise local laws. This traditional legal framework causes difficulty for commercial operators in the electronic marketplace who want to ensure that they comply with the large number of local laws which might apply to their activities. It is sometimes possible for operators to screen out users from particular countries,[48] but this is no panacea and alternative models of governance have been suggested. One such alternative is what the OECD has termed the "World Government Model".[49] Under this model, global rules would be established to regulate the electronic marketplace and a global authority would settle disputes. However, the constituent legal regimes of the world appear to be too heterogeneous to merge into one within the foreseeable future. Some countries have strong traditions of free speech, whilst others have strong traditions of protecting against libel, or commercially misleading speech. Some countries emphasise the role of the state as protector of the people, whilst others emphasise the right of freedom from governmental interference. These differences make it unlikely that any global and binding legal framework will be agreed in the near future, although a number of non-binding instruments have been agreed under the auspices of the United Nations,[50] the OECD,[51] and the

---

[47] See A. Page, "Self-regulation: the constitutional dimension", (1986) 49 *Modern Law Review* 141.

[48] In the case of websites, aside from asking visitors in which country they are based, operators can usually access the clocks of visitors' computers and via the relevant time zone can thus often make a reasonable guess as to the country, or at least the area, in which a visitor is situated.

[49] OECD Committee on Consumer Policy Background Paper to OECD International Forum, *Gateways to the Global Market: Consumers and Electronic Commerce* (Paris, 3–4 March 1997), at 25.

[50] See e.g. the Model Law on Electronic Commerce of the United Nations Commission on International Trade Law, <www.un.or.at/uncitral/>.

[51] See e.g. the OECD Privacy Guidelines in the Electronic Environment <www.oecd.org/subject/e_commerce>. Generally on the OECD's work see, "Electronic Commerce: opportunities and challenges for government" (the "Sacher Report"), (Paris, OECD, 1997), <www.oecd.org/dsti/sti/it/ec/act/sacher.htm>.

ICC,[52] and there can be little doubt that these instruments impact upon national law.[53]

A further alternative model of governance is that of the "Brave New World".[54] This model postulates self-regulation as the appropriate form of regulation for "cyberspace", on the basis that cyberspace is too far removed from the existing, bordered world to be subjected to its laws. The rationale behind this view is succinctly put by Johnson and Post:

> "Cyberspace radically undermines the relationship between legally significant (online) phenomena and physical location. The rise of the global computer network is destroying the link between geographical location and (1) the *power* of the local government to assert control over online behaviour; (2) the *effects* of online behaviour on individuals or things; (3) the *legitimacy* of the efforts of a local sovereign to enforce rules applicable to global phenomena; and (4) the ability of physical location to give notice of which sets of rules apply".[55]

In support of this thesis, it can be said that Internet users have for some time engaged in self-regulation. Those who send junk e-mail (also known as "spam") often find that offended recipients electronically attack the sender's computer system. Individuals can communicate easily using newsgroups, e-mail lists and websites. Instituting a system of self-regulation would continue this tradition and it would free governments from the burden of regulation.

The "Brave New World" model has parallels with the mediaeval Law Merchant, a regulatory system developed by traders in the light of their own expertise and needs, with little regard to national borders.[56] Yet the circumstances which surrounded the development of the Law Merchant differ from those which currently surround electronic commerce. Both states and public legal systems were undeveloped in the medieval period compared with today. Further, whilst the Law Merchant governed relationships between small numbers of traders who were known to each other, the law of the electronic marketplace governs a large, disparate and partly anonymous group of market actors. It can also be said that although electronic commerce undermines the relationship between legally significant online acts and physical location, the link is still there. Acts *are* both carried out, and more importantly impact, in identifiable physical locations.

---

[52] See e.g., International Chamber of Commerce, "General Usage for Digitally Ensured Commerce", <www.iccwbo.org/guidec2.htm>.

[53] A. Boss, "Electronic Commerce and the Symbiotic Relationship Between International and Domestic Law Reform", (1998) 72 *Tulane Law Review* 1931.

[54] Background Paper to the OECD International Forum, Gateways to the Global Market: Consumers and Electronic Commerce (Paris, 3–4 March 1997), at 25.

[55] D. Johnston and D. Post, "Law and Borders—The Rise of Law in Cyberspace", (1996) 48 *Stanford Law Review* 1367 (also <http://www.cli.org/>). See in a similar vein, J. Delacourt, "The International Impact of Internet Regulation", (1997) 38 *Harvard International Law Journal* 207. Contrast J. Goldsmith, "Against Cyberanarchy", (1998) 65 *University of Chicago Law Review* 1199. See also the site of the Internet Society at <www.isoc.org>. For an example of their activity in commenting on proposed legislation see <www.isoc.org/whatsnew/senateban.html>.

[56] D. Johnson and D. Post, n. 55 above.

Thus, neither the World Government Model nor the Brave New World Model offer viable alternative systems of regulation. As the Commission has recognised,[57] whilst globalisation is exerting its pull on electronic commerce, the role of the Community is a crucial one.

10.3 CONCLUDING SUMMARY

Community electronic commerce law exhibits the following characteristics:

(1) a lack of focus on the individual;
(2) an incompleteness, particularly in the area of enforcement and in the current lack of comprehensive regulation of copyright, electronic signatures, commercial communications;
(3) a lack of internal coherence;
(4) a rate of development which is slow in comparison to the phenomena it seeks to govern;
(5) a dominance over Member State law.

---

[57] Commission, *Communication on Globalisation and the Information Society—the need for strengthened international coordination* (COM(98) 50).

Glossary

Anonymous ftp site	An interactive service provided by a host computer permitting anyone to transfer data using File Transfer Protocol.
Central Repository	Public department or agency set up to act as a point of contact between a Trusted Third Party and law enforcement agencies.
Cryptographic key	A function used with a cryptographic algorithm to encrypt or decrypt data.
Cryptography	The science of keeping data secure.
Decryption	Converting encrypted data into intelligible form.
Digital Signature	Data appended to a message that ensures its source and integrity.
Domain name	The part of an electronic address that specifies the relevant computer systems e.g. in john.smith@test.com the domain name is "test".
Download	Send data from a typically large computer to a typically small one (usually a personal computer).
Electronic Data Interchange	Technology used to automate routine business transactions, such as re-ordering goods.
Electronic Funds Transfer	Payment completed electronically.
Electronic Signature	See "digital signature".
Email	"Electronic mail", is mail sent from one computer to another, usually comprising of simple text.
Encryption	Using a mathematical function to turn data into unintelligible code.
Frame	Part of a Web page which can be manipulated independently of the rest of the page, i.e. scrolled up and down.
Home page	The first page of a Website.

HTM(L)	Hyper Text Mark-up (Language), a standard format for documents on the Web.
HTTP:	Hyper Text Transfer Protocol: A protocol used to link Websites, "http" is the beginning of all Web addresses.
Hyperlink	A word or phrase found in a document on the Web that, when clicked on, will link to the document to which it refers.
Internet	A global network of computers which communicate on the basis of common technology, providing services such as email and the World Wide Web.
Key escrow / recovery	Allowing authorised persons, such as law enforcement agencies, to access a cryptographic key or keys in order to decrypt data.
Pretty Good Privacy (PGP)	An algorithm for public key encryption, available free on the Web.
Repository	A store for certificates guaranteeing the source and integrity of computer messages.
Server	A computer which "serves" other computers, for example by storing a Web page.
Trusted Third Party	A neutral third party in communication, such as an Internet Service Provider or a bank.
Upload	Send data from a typically small computer to a typically larger one.
Website	A document on a computer which can be accessed from all over the world via the Internet.
World Wide Web (or "Web")	A collection of documents made available using Internet communications technology.

Appendix 1

DIRECTIVE 97/7/EC OF THE *EUROPEAN PARLIAMENT* AND OF THE *COUNCIL* of 20 May 1997
On The Protection Of Consumers In Respect Of Distance Contracts

THE EUROPEAN PARLIAMENT AND THE COUNCIL OF THE EURO-PEAN UNION,

Having regard to the Treaty establishing the European Community, and in particular Article 100a thereof,

Having regard to the proposal from the Commission (1),

Having regard to the opinion of the Economic and Social Committee (2),

Acting in accordance with the procedure laid down in Article 189b of the Treaty (3), in the light of the joint text approved by the Conciliation Committee on 27 November 1996,

(1) Whereas, in connection with the attainment of the aims of the internal market, measures must be taken for the gradual consolidation of that market;

(2) Whereas the free movement of goods and services affects not only the business sector but also private individuals; whereas it means that consumers should be able to have access to the goods and services of another Member State on the same terms as the population of that State;

(3) Whereas, for consumers, cross-border distance selling could be one of the main tangible results of the completion of the internal market, as noted, inter alia, in the communication from the Commission to the Council entitled 'Towards a single market in distribution'; whereas it is essential to the smooth operation of the internal market for consumers to be able to have dealings with a business outside their country, even if it has a subsidiary in the consumer's country of residence;

(4) Whereas the introduction of new technologies is increasing the number of ways for consumers to obtain information about offers anywhere in the Community and to place orders; whereas some Member States have already taken different or diverging measures to protect consumers in respect of distance selling, which has had a detrimental effect on competition between businesses in the internal market; whereas it is therefore necessary to introduce at Community level a minimum set of common rules in this area;

(5) Whereas paragraphs 18 and 19 of the Annex to the Council resolution of 14 April 1975 on a preliminary programme of the European Economic Community for a consumer protection and information policy (4) point to the

need to protect the purchasers of goods or services from demands for payment for unsolicited goods and from high-pressure selling methods;

(6) Whereas paragraph 33 of the communication from the Commission to the Council entitled 'A new impetus for consumer protection policy', which was approved by the Council resolution of 23 June 1986 (5), states that the Commission will submit proposals regarding the use of new information technologies enabling consumers to place orders with suppliers from their homes;

(7) Whereas the Council resolution of 9 November 1989 on future priorities for relaunching consumer protection policy (6) calls upon the Commission to give priority to the areas referred to in the Annex to that resolution; whereas that Annex refers to new technologies involving teleshopping; whereas the Commission has responded to that resolution by adopting a three-year action plan for consumer protection policy in the European Economic Community (1990–1992); whereas that plan provides for the adoption of a Directive;

(8) Whereas the languages used for distance contracts are a matter for the Member States;

(9) Whereas contracts negotiated at a distance involve the use of one or more means of distance communication; whereas the various means of communication are used as part of an organized distance sales or service-provision scheme not involving the simultaneous presence of the supplier and the consumer; whereas the constant development of those means of communication does not allow an exhaustive list to be compiled but does require principles to be defined which are valid even for those which are not as yet in widespread use;

(10) Whereas the same transaction comprising successive operations or a series of separate operations over a period of time may give rise to different legal descriptions depending on the law of the Member States; whereas the provisions of this Directive cannot be applied differently according to the law of the Member States, subject to their recourse to Article 14; whereas, to that end, there is therefore reason to consider that there must at least be compliance with the provisions of this Directive at the time of the first of a series of successive operations or the first of a series of separate operations over a period of time which may be considered as forming a whole, whether that operation or series of operations are the subject of a single contract or successive, separate contracts;

(11) Whereas the use of means of distance communication must not lead to a reduction in the information provided to the consumer; whereas the information that is required to be sent to the consumer should therefore be determined, whatever the means of communication used; whereas the information supplied must also comply with the other relevant Community rules, in particular those in Council Directive 84/450/EEC of 10 September 1984 relating to the approximation of the laws, regulations and administrative provisions of the Member States concerning misleading advertising (7); whereas, if exceptions are made to the obligation to provide information, it is up to the consumer, on a discre-

tionary basis, to request certain basic information such as the identity of the supplier, the main characteristics of the goods or services and their price;

(12) Whereas in the case of communication by telephone it is appropriate that the consumer receive enough information at the beginning of the conversation to decide whether or not to continue;

(13) Whereas information disseminated by certain electronic technologies is often ephemeral in nature insofar as it is not received on a permanent medium; whereas the consumer must therefore receive written notice in good time of the information necessary for proper performance of the contract;

(14) Whereas the consumer is not able actually to see the product or ascertain the nature of the service provided before concluding the contract; whereas provision should be made, unless otherwise specified in this Directive, for a right of withdrawal from the contract; whereas, if this right is to be more than formal, the costs, if any, borne by the consumer when exercising the right of withdrawal must be limited to the direct costs for returning the goods; whereas this right of withdrawal shall be without prejudice to the consumer's rights under national laws, with particular regard to the receipt of damaged products and services or of products and services not corresponding to the description given in the offer of such products or services; whereas it is for the Member States to determine the other conditions and arrangements following exercise of the right of withdrawal;

(15) Whereas it is also necessary to prescribe a time limit for performance of the contract if this is not specified at the time of ordering;

(16) Whereas the promotional technique involving the dispatch of a product or the provision of a service to the consumer in return for payment without a prior request from, or the explicit agreement of, the consumer cannot be permitted, unless a substitute product or service is involved;

(17) Whereas the principles set out in Articles 8 and 10 of the European Convention for the Protection of Human Rights and Fundamental Freedoms of 4 November 1950 apply; whereas the consumer's right to privacy, particularly as regards freedom from certain particularly intrusive means of communication, should be recognized; whereas specific limits on the use of such means should therefore be stipulated; whereas Member States should take appropriate measures to protect effectively those consumers, who do not wish to be contacted through certain means of communication, against such contacts, without prejudice to the particular safeguards available to the consumer under Community legislation concerning the protection of personal data and privacy;

(18) Whereas it is important for the minimum binding rules contained in this Directive to be supplemented where appropriate by voluntary arrangements among the traders concerned, in line with Commission recommendation 92/295/EEC of 7 April 1992 on codes of practice for the protection of consumers in respect of contracts negotiated at a distance (8);

(19) Whereas in the interest of optimum consumer protection it is important for consumers to be satisfactorily informed of the provisions of this Directive and of codes of practice that may exist in this field;

(20) Whereas non-compliance with this Directive may harm not only consumers but also competitors; whereas provisions may therefore be laid down enabling public bodies or their representatives, or consumer organizations which, under national legislation, have a legitimate interest in consumer protection, or professional organizations which have a legitimate interest in taking action, to monitor the application thereof;

(21) Whereas it is important, with a view to consumer protection, to address the question of cross-border complaints as soon as this is feasible; whereas the Commission published on 14 February 1996 a plan of action on consumer access to justice and the settlement of consumer disputes in the internal market; whereas that plan of action includes specific initiatives to promote out-of-court procedures; whereas objective criteria (Annex II) are suggested to ensure the reliability of those procedures and provision is made for the use of standardized claims forms (Annex III);

(22) Whereas in the use of new technologies the consumer is not in control of the means of communication used; whereas it is therefore necessary to provide that the burden of proof may be on the supplier;

(23) Whereas there is a risk that, in certain cases, the consumer may be deprived of protection under this Directive through the designation of the law of a non-member country as the law applicable to the contract; whereas provisions should therefore be included in this Directive to avert that risk;

(24) Whereas a Member State may ban, in the general interest, the marketing on its territory of certain goods and services through distance contracts; whereas that ban must comply with Community rules; whereas there is already provision for such bans, notably with regard to medicinal products, under Council Directive 89/552/EEC of 3 October 1989 on the co-ordination of certain provisions laid down by law, regulation or administrative action in Member States concerning the pursuit of television broadcasting activities (9) and Council Directive 92/28/EEC of 31 March 1992 on the advertising of medicinal products for human use (10),

HAVE ADOPTED THIS DIRECTIVE:

Article 1
Object

The object of this Directive is to approximate the laws, regulations and administrative provisions of the Member States concerning distance contracts between consumers and suppliers.

Article 2
Definitions

For the purposes of this Directive:

(1) '*distance contract*' means any contract concerning goods or services concluded between a supplier and a consumer under an organized distance sales or

service-provision scheme run by the supplier, who, for the purpose of the contract, makes exclusive use of one or more means of distance communication up to and including the moment at which the contract is concluded;

(2) *'consumer'* means any natural person who, in contracts covered by this Directive, is acting for purposes which are outside his trade, business or profession;

(3) *'supplier'* means any natural or legal person who, in contracts covered by this Directive, is acting in his commercial or professional capacity;

(4) *'means of distance communication'* means any means which, without the simultaneous physical presence of the supplier and the consumer, may be used for the conclusion of a contract between those parties. An indicative list of the means covered by this Directive is contained in Annex I;

(5) *'operator of a means of communication'* means any public or private natural or legal person whose trade, business or profession involves making one or more means of distance communication available to suppliers.

Article 3
Exemptions

1. This Directive shall not apply to contracts:

— relating to financial services, a non-exhaustive list of which is given in Annex II,
— concluded by means of automatic vending machines or automated commercial premises,
— concluded with telecommunications operators through the use of public pay phones,
— concluded for the construction and sale of immovable property or relating to other immovable property rights, except for rental,
— concluded at an auction.

2. Articles 4, 5, 6 and 7 (1) shall not apply:

— to contracts for the supply of foodstuffs, beverages or other goods intended for everyday consumption supplied to the home of the consumer, to his residence or to his workplace by regular rounds men,
— to contracts for the provision of accommodation, transport, catering or leisure services, where the supplier undertakes, when the contract is concluded, to provide these services on a specific date or within a specific period; exceptionally, in the case of outdoor leisure events, the supplier can reserve the right not to apply Article 7 (2) in specific circumstances.

Article 4
Prior information

1. In good time prior to the conclusion of any distance contract, the consumer shall be provided with the following information:

(a) the identity of the supplier and, in the case of contracts requiring payment in advance, his address;

(b) the main characteristics of the goods or services;

(c) the price of the goods or services including all taxes;

(d) delivery costs, where appropriate;

(e) the arrangements for payment, delivery or performance;

(f) the existence of a right of withdrawal, except in the cases referred to in Article 6 (3);

(g) the cost of using the means of distance communication, where it is calculated other than at the basic rate;

(h) the period for which the offer or the price remains valid;

(i) where appropriate, the minimum duration of the contract in the case of contracts for the supply of products or services to be performed permanently or recurrently.

2. The information referred to in paragraph 1, the commercial purpose of which must be made clear, shall be provided in a clear and comprehensible manner in any way appropriate to the means of distance communication used, with due regard, in particular, to the principles of good faith in commercial transactions, and the principles governing the protection of those who are unable, pursuant to the legislation of the Member States, to give their consent, such as minors.

3. Moreover, in the case of telephone communications, the identity of the supplier and the commercial purpose of the call shall be made explicitly clear at the beginning of any conversation with the consumer.

Article 5
Written confirmation of information

1. The consumer must receive written confirmation or confirmation in another durable medium available and accessible to him of the information referred to in Article 4 (1) (a) to (f), in good time during the performance of the contract, and at the latest at the time of delivery where goods not for delivery to third parties are concerned, unless the information has already been given to the consumer prior to conclusion of the contract in writing or on another durable medium available and accessible to him.

In any event the following must be provided:

— written information on the conditions and procedures for exercising the right of withdrawal, within the meaning of Article 6, including the cases referred to in the first indent of Article 6 (3),

— the geographical address of the place of business of the supplier to which the consumer may address any complaints,

— information on after-sales services and guarantees which exist,

— the conclusion for cancelling the contract, where it is of unspecified duration or a duration exceeding one year.

2. Paragraph 1 shall not apply to services which are performed through the use of a means of distance communication, where they are supplied on only one occasion and are invoiced by the operator of the means of distance communication. Nevertheless, the consumer must in all cases be able to obtain the geographical address of the place of business of the supplier to which he may address any complaints.

Article 6
Right of withdrawal

1. For any distance contract the consumer shall have a period of at least seven working days in which to withdraw from the contract without penalty and without giving any reason. The only charge that may be made to the consumer because of the exercise of his right of withdrawal is the direct cost of returning the goods.

The period for exercise of this right shall begin:

— in the case of goods, from the day of receipt by the consumer where the obligations laid down in Article 5 have been fulfilled,
— in the case of services, from the day of conclusion of the contract or from the day on which the obligations laid down in Article 5 were fulfilled if they are fulfilled after conclusion of the contract, provided that this period does not exceed the three-month period referred to in the following subparagraph.

If the supplier has failed to fulfil the obligations laid down in Article 5, the period shall be three months. The period shall begin:

— in the case of goods, from the day of receipt by the consumer,
— in the case of services, from the day of conclusion of the contract.

If the information referred to in Article 5 is supplied within this three-month period, the seven working day period referred to in the first subparagraph shall begin as from that moment.

2. Where the right of withdrawal has been exercised by the consumer pursuant to this Article, the supplier shall be obliged to reimburse the sums paid by the consumer free of charge. The only charge that may be made to the consumer because of the exercise of his right of withdrawal is the direct cost of returning the goods. Such reimbursement must be carried out as soon as possible and in any case within 30 days.

3. Unless the parties have agreed otherwise, the consumer may not exercise the right of withdrawal provided for in paragraph 1 in respect of contracts:

— for the provision of services if performance has begun, with the consumer's agreement, before the end of the seven working day period referred to in paragraph 1,
— for the supply of goods or services the price of which is dependent on fluctuations in the financial market which cannot be controlled by the supplier,

— for the supply of goods made to the consumer's specifications or clearly personalized or which, by reason of their nature, cannot be returned or are liable to deteriorate or expire rapidly,

— for the supply of audio or video recordings or computer software which were unsealed by the consumer,

— for the supply of newspapers, periodicals and magazines,

— for gaming and lottery services.

4. The Member States shall make provision in their legislation to ensure that:

— if the price of goods or services is fully or partly covered by credit granted by the supplier, or

— if that price is fully or partly covered by credit granted to the consumer by a third party on the basis of an agreement between the third party and the supplier,

the credit agreement shall be cancelled, without any penalty, if the consumer exercises his right to withdraw from the contract in accordance with paragraph 1.

Member States shall determine the detailed rules for cancellation of the credit agreement.

Article 7
Performance

1. Unless the parties have agreed otherwise, the supplier must execute the order within a maximum of 30 days from the day following that on which the consumer forwarded his order to the supplier.

2. Where a supplier fails to perform his side of the contract on the grounds that the goods or services ordered are unavailable, the consumer must be informed of this situation and must be able to obtain a refund of any sums he has paid as soon as possible and in any case within 30 days.

3. Nevertheless, Member States may lay down that the supplier may provide the consumer with goods or services of equivalent quality and price provided that this possibility was provided for prior to the conclusion of the contract or in the contract. The consumer shall be informed of this possibility in a clear and comprehensible manner. The cost of returning the goods following exercise of the right of withdrawal shall, in this case, be borne by the supplier, and the consumer must be informed of this. In such cases the supply of goods or services may not be deemed to constitute inertia selling within the meaning of Article 9.

Article 8
Payment by card

Member States shall ensure that appropriate measures exist to allow a consumer:

— to request cancellation of a payment where fraudulent use has been made of his payment card in connection with distance contracts covered by this Directive,

— in the event of fraudulent use, to be recredited with the sums paid or have them returned.

Article 9
Inertia selling

Member States shall take the measures necessary to:

— prohibit the supply of goods or services to a consumer without their being ordered by the consumer beforehand, where such supply involves a demand for payment,
— exempt the consumer from the provision of any consideration in cases of unsolicited supply, the absence of a response not constituting consent.

Article 10
Restrictions on the use of certain means of distance communication

1. Use by a supplier of the following means requires the prior consent of the consumer:

— automated calling system without human intervention (automatic calling machine),
— facsimile machine (fax).

2. Member States shall ensure that means of distance communication, other than those referred to in paragraph 1, which allow individual communications may be used only where there is no clear objection from the consumer.

Article 11
Judicial or administrative redress

1. Member States shall ensure that adequate and effective means exist to ensure compliance with this Directive in the interests of consumers.
2. The means referred to in paragraph 1 shall include provisions whereby one or more of the following bodies, as determined by national law, may take action under national law before the courts or before the competent administrative bodies to ensure that the national provisions for the implementation of this Directive are applied:

(a) public bodies or their representatives;
(b) consumer organizations having a legitimate interest in protecting consumers;
(c) professional organizations having a legitimate interest in acting.

3. (a) Member States may stipulate that the burden of proof concerning the existence of prior information, written confirmation, compliance with time-limits or consumer consent can be placed on the supplier.
(b) Member States shall take the measures needed to ensure that suppliers and operators of means of communication, where they are able to do so, cease practices which do not comply with measures adopted pursuant to this Directive.

4. Member States may provide for voluntary supervision by self-regulatory bodies of compliance with the provisions of this Directive and recourse to such bodies for the settlement of disputes to be added to the means which Member States must provided to ensure compliance with the provisions of this Directive.

Article 12
Binding nature

1. The consumer may not waive the rights conferred on him by the transposition of this Directive into national law.

2. Member States shall take the measures needed to ensure that the consumer does not lose the protection granted by this Directive by virtue of the choice of the law of a non-member country as the law applicable to the contract if the latter has close connection with the territory of one or more Member States.

Article 13
Community rules

1. The provisions of this Directive shall apply insofar as there are no particular provisions in rules of Community law governing certain types of distance contracts in their entirety.
2. Where specific Community rules contain provisions governing only certain aspects of the supply of goods or provision of services, those provisions, rather than the provisions of this Directive, shall apply to these specific aspects of the distance contracts.

Article 14
Minimal clause

Member States may introduce or maintain, in the area covered by this Directive, more stringent provisions compatible with the Treaty, to ensure a higher level of consumer protection. Such provisions shall, where appropriate, include a ban, in the general interest, on the marketing of certain goods or services, particularly medicinal products, within their territory by means of distance contracts, with due regard for the Treaty.

Article 15
Implementation

1. Member States shall bring into force the laws, regulations and administrative provisions necessary to comply with this Directive no later than three years after it enters into force. They shall forthwith inform the Commission thereof.
2. When Member States adopt the measures referred to in paragraph 1, these shall contain a reference to this Directive or shall be accompanied by such reference on the occasion of their official publication. The procedure for such reference shall be laid down by Member States.

3. Member States shall communicate to the Commission the text of the provisions of national law which they adopt in the field governed by this Directive.

4. No later than four years after the entry into force of this Directive the Commission shall submit a report to the European Parliament and the Council on the implementation of this Directive, accompanied if appropriate by a proposal for the revision thereof.

Article 16
Consumer information

Member States shall take appropriate measures to inform the consumer of the national law transposing this Directive and shall encourage, where appropriate, professional organizations to inform consumers of their codes of practice.

Article 17
Complaints systems

The Commission shall study the feasibility of establishing effective means to deal with consumers' complaints in respect of distance selling. Within two years after the entry into force of this Directive the Commission shall submit a report to the European Parliament and the Council on the results of the studies, accompanied if appropriate by proposals.

Article 18

This Directive shall enter into force on the day of its publication in the Official Journal of the European Communities.

Article 19

This Directive is addressed to the Member States.

Done at Brussels, 20 May 1997.
For the European Parliament
The President

J.M. GIL-ROBLES

For the Council
The President

J. VAN AARTSEN

Published in OJ No. 166, 04.06.1997
To annex

---

(1) OJ No C 156, 23. 6. 1992, p. 14 and OJ No C 308, 15. 11. 1993, p. 18.
(2) OJ No C 19, 25. 1. 1993, p. 111.
(3) Opinion of the European Parliament of 26 May 1993 (OJ No C 176, 28. 6.

1993, p. 95), Council common position of 29 June 1995 (OJ No C 288, 30. 10. 1995, p. 1) and Decision of the European Parliament of 13 December 1995 (OJ No C 17, 22. 1. 1996, p. 51). Decision of the European Parliament of 16 January 1997 and Council Decision of 20 January 1997.

(4) OJ No C 92, 25. 4. 1975, p. 1.
(5) OJ No C 167, 5. 7. 1986, p. 1.
(6) OJ No C 294, 22. 11. 1989, p. 1.
(7) OJ No L 250, 19. 9. 1984, p. 17.
(8) OJ No L 156, 10. 6. 1992, p. 21.
(9) OJ No L 298, 17. 10. 1989, p. 23.
(10) OJ No L 113, 30. 4. 1992, p. 13.
(11)
(12) OJ No C 19, 25. 1. 1993, p. 111.
(13)
(14) OJ No C 92, 25. 4. 1975, p. 1.
(15) OJ No C 167, 5. 7. 1986, p. 1.
(16) OJ No C 294, 22. 11. 1989, p. 1.
(17) OJ No L 250, 19. 9. 1984, p. 17.
(18) OJ No L 156, 10. 6. 1992, p. 21.
(19) OJ No L 298, 17. 10. 1989, p. 23.
(20) OJ No L 113, 30. 4. 1992, p. 13.

ANNEX I
Means of communication covered by Article 2 (4)

— Unaddressed printed matter
— Addressed printed matter
— Standard letter
— Press advertising with order form
— Catalogue
— Telephone with human intervention
— Telephone without human intervention (automatic calling machine, audio-text)
— Radio
— Videophone (telephone with screen)
— Videotex (microcomputer and television screen) with keyboard or touch screen
— Electronic mail
— Facsimile machine (fax)
— Television (teleshopping).

ANNEX II
Financial services within the meaning of Article 3 (1)

— Investment services
— Insurance and reinsurance operations
— Banking services
— Operations relating to dealings in futures or options.

Such services include in particular:

— investment services referred to in the Annex to Directive 93/22/EEC (1); services of collective investment undertakings,
— services covered by the activities subject to mutual recognition referred to in the Annex to Directive 89/646/EEC (2);
— operations covered by the insurance and reinsurance activities referred to in:
— Article 1 of Directive 73/239/EEC (3),
— the Annex to Directive 79/267/EEC (4),
— Directive 64/225/EEC (5),
— Directives 92/49/EEC (6) and 92/96/EEC (7).

---

(1) OJ No L 141, 11. 6. 1993, p. 27.
(2) OJ No L 386, 30. 12. 1989, p. 1. Directive as amended by Directive 92/30/EEC (OJ No L 110, 28. 4. 1992, p. 52).
(3) OJ No L 228, 16. 8. 1973, p. 3. Directive as last amended by Directive 92/49/EEC (OJ No L 228, 11. 8. 1992, p. 1).
(4) OJ No L 63, 13. 3. 1979, p. 1. Directive as last amended by Directive 90/619/EEC (OJ No L 330, 29. 11. 1990, p. 50).
(5) OJ No 56, 4. 4. 1964, p. 878/64. Directive as amended by the 1973 Act of Accession.
(6) OJ No L 228, 11. 8. 1992, p. 1.
(7) OJ No L 360, 9. 12. 1992, p. 1.

Appendix 2

Proposal for a
EUROPEAN PARLIAMENT AND COUNCIL DIRECTIVE
on certain legal aspects of electronic commerce in the internal market

CHAPTER V   ADVISORY COMMITTEE AND FINAL PROVISIONS
Article 23   Committee
Article 24   Re-examination
Article 25   Implementation
Article 26   Entry into force
Article 27   Addressees

ANNEX I   (activities excluded from the scope of application of the Directive)
ANNEX II   (derogations from Article 3)

Proposal for a
EUROPEAN PARLIAMENT AND COUNCIL DIRECTIVE
on certain legal aspects of electronic commerce in the internal market

THE EUROPEAN PARLIAMENT AND THE COUNCIL OF THE EURO-PEAN UNION,

Having regard to the Treaty establishing the European Community, and in particular Articles 57(2), 66 and 100a thereof,

Having regard to the proposal from the Commission[1],

Having regard to the opinion of the Economic and Social Committee[2],

Acting in accordance with the procedure referred to in Article 189b of the Treaty[3],

(1)   Whereas the European Union is seeking to forge ever closer links between the States and peoples of Europe, to ensure economic and social progress; whereas, in accordance with Article 7a of the Treaty, the internal market comprises an area without internal frontiers in which the free movement of goods, services and the freedom of establishment are ensured; whereas the development of Information Society services within the area without internal frontiers is vital to eliminating the barriers which divide the European peoples;

(2)   Whereas the development of electronic commerce within the Information Society offers significant employment opportunities in the Community, particularly in small and medium-sized enterprises, and will stimulate economic growth and investment in innovation by European companies;

(3)   Whereas Information Society services span a wide range of economic activities which can, in particular, consist of selling goods on line;

[1] OJ C.
[2] OJ C.
[3] OJ C.

whereas they are not solely restricted to services giving rise to on-line contracting but also, in so far as they represent an economic activity, extend to services which are not remunerated by those who receive them, such as those offering on-line information; whereas Information Society services also include on-line activities via telephony and telefax;

(4) Whereas the development of Information Society services within the Community is restricted by a number of legal obstacles to the proper functioning of the internal market which hamper or make less attractive the exercise of the freedom of establishment and the freedom to provide services; whereas these obstacles arise from divergences in legislation and from the legal uncertainty as to which national rules apply to such services; whereas, in the absence of coordination and adjustment of legislation in the relevant areas, obstacles might be justified in the light of the case-law of the Court of Justice of the European Communities; whereas legal uncertainty exists with regard to the extent to which Member States may control services originating from another Member State;

(5) Whereas, in the light of Community objectives, of Articles 52 and 59 of the Treaty and of secondary Community law, these obstacles should be eliminated by coordinating certain national laws and by clarifying certain legal concepts at Community level to the extent necessary for the proper functioning of the internal market; whereas, by dealing only with certain specific matters which give rise to problems for the internal market, this Directive is fully consistent with the need to respect the principle of subsidiarity as set out in Article 3b of the Treaty;

(6) Whereas, in accordance with the principle of proportionality, the measures provided for in this Directive are strictly limited to the minimum needed to achieve the objective of the proper functioning of the internal market; whereas, where action at Community level is necessary, and in order to guarantee an area which is truly without internal frontiers as far as electronic commerce is concerned, the Directive must ensure a high level of protection of objectives of general interest, in particular consumer protection and the protection of public health; whereas according to Article 129 of the Treaty, the protection of public health is an essential component of other Community policies; whereas this Directive does not impact on the legal requirements applicable to the delivery of goods as such, nor those applicable to services which are not Information Society services;

(7) Whereas this Directive does not aim to establish specific rules on international private law relating to conflicts of law or jurisdiction and is therefore without prejudice to the relevant international conventions;

(8) Whereas Information Society services should be supervised at the source of the activity, in order to ensure an effective protection of public interest

objectives; whereas, to that end, it is necessary to ensure that the competent authority provides such protection not only for the citizens of its own country but for all Community citizens; whereas, moreover, in order to effectively guarantee freedom to provide services and legal certainty for suppliers and recipients of services, such Information Society services should only be subject to the law of the Member State in which the service provider is established; whereas, in order to improve mutual trust between Member States, it is essential to state clearly this responsibility on the part of the Member State whence the services orginate;

(9)   Whereas the place at which a service provider is established should be determined in accordance with the case-law of the Court of Justice; whereas the place of establishment of a company providing services via an internet website is not the place at which the technology supporting its website is located or the place at which its website is accessible; whereas, where the same supplier has a number of establishments, the competent Member State will be the one in which the supplier has the centre of his activities; whereas in cases where it is particularly difficult to assess in which Member States the supplier is established, cooperative procedures should be established between the Member States and the consultative committee should be capable of being convened in urgent cases to examine such difficulties;

(10)   Whereas commercial communications are essential for the financing of Information Society services and for developing a wide variety of new, chargefree services; whereas in the interests of consumer protection and fair trading, commercial communications, including discounts, promotional offers and promotional competitions, must meet a number of transparency requirements and that these requirements are without prejudice to Directive 97/7/EC of the European Parliament and of the Council on the protection of consumers in respect of distance contracts[4]; whereas this Directive should not affect existing directives on commercial communications, in particular Directive 98/43/EC of the European Parliament and of the Council[5] on tobacco advertising;

(11)   Whereas Article 10(2) of Directive 97/7/EC and Article 12(2) of European Parliament and Council Directive 97/66/EC of 15 December 1997 concerning the processing of personal data and the protection of privacy in the telecommunications sector[6] address the issue of consent by receivers to certain forms of unsolicited commercial communication and are fully applicable to Information Society services;

(12)   Whereas, in order to remove barriers to the development of cross-border services within the Community which professional practitioners might

---

[4] OJ L 144, 4.6.1997, p. 19.
[5] OJ L 213, 30.7.1998, p. 9.
[6] OJ L 24, 30.1.1998, p. 1.

offer on the internet, it is necessary that compliance be guaranteed at Community level with professional rules aiming, in particular, to protect consumers or public health; whereas codes of conduct at Community level would be the best means of determining the rules on professional ethics applicable to commercial communication; whereas the drawingup or, where appropriate, the adaptation of such rules should in the first place be encouraged by, rather than laid down in, this Directive; whereas the regulated professional activities governed by this Directive should be understood in the light of the definition set out in Article 1(d) of Council Directive 89/48/EEC of 21 December 1988 on a general system for the recognition of higher-education diplomas awarded on completion of professional education and training of at least three years' duration[7];

(13)   Whereas each Member State should amend its legislation containing requirements, and in particular requirements as to form, which are likely to curb the use of contracts by electronic means, subject to any Community measure in the field of taxation that could be adopted on electronic invoicing; whereas the examination of the legislation requiring such adjustment should be systematic and should cover all the necessary stages and acts of the contractual process, including the filing of the contract; whereas the result of this amendment should be to make contracts concluded electronically genuinely and effectively workable in law and in practice; whereas the legal effect of electronic signatures is dealt with by European Parliament and Council Directive 99/.../EC [on a common framework for electronic signatures][8]; whereas it is necessary to clarify at what point in time a contract entered into electronically is considered to be actually concluded; whereas the service recipient's agreement to enter into a contract may take the form of an online payment; whereas the acknowledgment of receipt by a service provider may take the form of the online provision of the service paid for;

(14)   Whereas, amongst others, Council Directive 93/13/EEC[9] regarding unfair contract terms and Directive 97/7/EC, form a vital element for protecting consumers in contractual matters; whereas those directives also apply in their entirety to Information Society services; whereas that same Community *acquis* also embraces Council Directive 84/450/EEC[10] on misleading advertising, as amended by European Parliament and Council Directive 97/55/EC[11], Council Directive 87/102/EEC[12] on consumer credit; as last amended by European Parliament and Council

---

[7]   OJ L 19, 24.1.1989, p. 16.
[8]   COM(1998) 297 final, 13.5.1998.
[9]   OJ L 95, 21.4.1993, p. 29.
[10]   OJ L 250, 19.9.1984, p. 17.
[11]   OJ L 290, 23.10.1997, p. 18.
[12]   OJ L 42, 12.2.1987, p. 48.

Directive 98/7/EC[13], Council Directive 90/314/EEC[14] on package travel, package holidays and package tours, and European Parliament and Council Directive 98/6/EC[15] on the indication of prices of products offered to consumers; whereas this Directive should be without prejudice to Directive 98/43/EC, adopted within the framework of the internal market, or to other directives on the protection of public health;

(15)   Whereas the confidentiality of electronic messages is guaranteed by Article 5 of Directive 97/66/EC; whereas in accordance with that Directive Member States must prohibit any kind of interception or surveillance of such electronic messages by others than the senders and receivers;

(16)   Whereas both existing and emerging disparities in Member States' legislation and caselaw concerning civil and criminal liability of service providers acting as intermediaries prevent the smooth functioning of the Internal Market, in particular by impairing the development of cross-border services and producing distortions of competition; whereas service providers have a duty to act, under certain circumstances, with a view to preventing or ceasing illegal activities; whereas the provisions of this Directive should constitute the appropriate basis for the development of rapid and reliable procedures for removing and disabling access to illegal information; whereas such mechanisms could be developed on the basis of voluntary agreements between all parties concerned; whereas it is in the interest of all parties involved in the provision of Information Society services to adopt and implement such procedures; whereas the provisions of this Directive relating to liability should not preclude the development and effective operation, by the different interested parties, of technical systems of protection and identification;

(17)   Whereas each Member State should be required, where necessary, to amend any legislation which is liable to hamper the use of schemes for the outofcourt settlement of disputes through electronic channels; whereas the result of this amendment must be to make the functioning of such schemes genuinely and effectively possible in law and in practice, even across borders; whereas the bodies responsible for such out-of-court settlement of consumer disputes must comply with certain essential principles, as set out in Commission Recommendation 98/257/EC of 30 March 1998 on the principles applicable to the bodies responsible for such settlement of consumer disputes[16];

(18)   Whereas it is necessary to exclude certain activities from the scope of this Directive, on the grounds that the freedom to provide services in these fields cannot, at this stage, be guaranteed under the Treaty or existing

---

[13]   OJ L 101, 1.4.1998, p. 17.
[14]   OJ L 158, 23.6.1990, p. 59.
[15]   OJ L 80, 18.3.1998, p. 27.
[16]   OJ L 115, 17.4.1998, p. 31.

secondary legislation; whereas excluding these activities does not preclude any instruments which might prove necessary for the proper functioning of the internal market; whereas taxation, particularly value-added tax imposed on a large number of the services covered by this Directive, must be excluded from the scope of this Directive; whereas, in this respect, the Commission also intends to extend the application of the principle of taxation at source to the provision of services within the Internal Market, thus giving its approach a general coherence;

(19) Whereas as regards the derogation contained in this Directive regarding contractual obligations concerning contracts concluded by consumers, those obligations should be interpreted as including information on the essential elements of the content of the contract, including consumer rights, which have a determining influence on the decision to contract;

(20) Whereas this Directive should not apply to services supplied by service providers established in a third country; whereas, in view of the global dimension of electronic commerce, it is, however, appropriate to ensure that the Community rules are consistent with international rules; whereas this Directive is without prejudice to the results of discussions within international organisations (WTO, OECD, UNCITRAL) on legal issues; whereas this Directive should also be without prejudice to the discussions within the Global Business Dialogue which were launched on the basis of the Commission Communication of 4 February 1998 on "Globalisation and the Information Society—The need for strengthened international coordination"[17];

(21) Whereas the Member States need to ensure, that, when Community acts are transposed into national legislation, Community law is duly applied with the same effectiveness and thoroughness as national law;

(22) Whereas the adoption of this Directive will not prevent the Member States from taking into account the various social, societal and cultural implications which are inherent in the advent of the Information Society nor hinder cultural, and notably audiovisual, policy measures, which the Member States might adopt, in conformity with Community law, taking into account their linguistic diversity, national and regional specificities and their cultural heritage; whereas, in any case, the development of the Information Society must ensure that Community citizens can have access to the cultural European heritage provided in the digital environment;

(23) Whereas the Council, in its Resolution of 3 November 1998 on the consumer aspects of the Information Society, stressed that the protection of consumers deserved special attention in this field; whereas the Commission will examine the degree to which existing consumer protection rules provide insufficient protection in the context of the Information

---

[17] COM(98) 50 final.

Society and will identify, where necessary, the deficiencies of this legislation and those issues which could require additional measures; whereas, if need be, the Commission should make specific additional proposals to resolve such deficiencies that will thereby have been identified;

(24)   Whereas this Directive should be without prejudice to Council Regulation (EEC) No 2299/89 of 24 July 1989 on a code of conduct for computerized reservation systems[18], as amended by Regulation (EEC) No 3089/93[19].

(25)   Whereas Commission Regulation (EC) No 2027/97[20] and the Warsaw Convention of 12 October 1929 place various obligations upon air carriers regarding the provision of information to their passengers, including information about the liability of the carrier; whereas this Directive is without prejudice to the requirements of those instruments,

HAVE ADOPTED THIS DIRECTIVE:

CHAPTER I
GENERAL PROVISIONS
Article 1
Objective and scope

1.   This Directive seeks to ensure the proper functioning of the internal market, particularly the free movement of Information Society services between the Member States.

2.   This Directive approximates, to the extent necessary for the achievement of the objective set out in paragraph 1, national provisions on Information Society services relating to the internal market arrangements, the establishment of service providers, commercial communications, electronic contracts, the liability of intermediaries, codes of conduct, out-of-court dispute settlements, court actions and cooperation between Member States.

3.   This Directive complements Community law applicable to Information Society services without prejudice to the existing level of protection for public health and consumer interests, as established by Community acts, including those adopted for the functioning of the Internal Market.

---

[18] OJ L 220, 29.7.1989, p. 1.
[19] OJ L 278, 11.11.1993, p. 1.
[20] OJ L 285, 17.10.1997, p. 1.

Article 2
Definitions

For the purpose of this Directive, the following terms shall bear the following meanings:

(a) *"Information Society services"*: any service normally provided for remuneration, at a distance, by electronic means and at the individual request of a recipient of services;
For the purpose of this definition:

—"at a distance" means that the service is provided without the parties being simultaneously present;
—"by electronic means" means that a service is sent initially and received at its destination by means of electronic equipment for the processing (including digital compression) and storage of data, and entirely transmitted, conveyed and received by wire, by radio, by optical means or by other electromagnetic means;
—"at the individual request of a recipient of services" means a service provided through the transmission of data on individual request.

(b) *"service provider"*: any natural or legal person providing an Information Society service;

(c) *"established service provider"*: a service provider who effectively pursues an economic activity using a fixed establishment for an indeterminate duration. The presence and use of the technical means and technologies required to provide the service do not constitute an establishment of the provider;

(d) *"recipient of the service"*: any natural or legal person who, for professional ends or otherwise, uses an Information Society service, in particular for the purposes of seeking information or making it accessible;

(e) *"commercial communications"*: any form of communication designed to promote, directly or indirectly, the goods, services or image of a company, organisation or person pursuing a commercial, industrial or craft activity or exercising a liberal profession. The following do not as such constitute commercial communications:

—information allowing direct access to the activity of the company, organisation or person, in particular a domain name or an electronicmail address,
—communications relating to the goods, services or image of the company, organisation or person compiled in an independent manner, in particular without financial consideration.

(f) *"coordinated field"*: the requirements applicable to Information Society service providers and Information Society services.

Article 3
Internal market

1. Each Member State shall ensure that the Information Society services provided by a service provider established on its territory comply with the national provisions applicable in the Member State in question which fall within this Directive's coordinated field.

2. Member States may not, for reasons falling within this Directive's coordinated field, restrict the freedom to provide Information Society services from another Member State.

3. Paragraph 1 shall cover the provisions set out in Articles 9, 10 and 11 only in so far as the law of the Member State applies by virtue of its rules of international private law.

CHAPTER II
PRINCIPLES
Section 1: Establishment and information requirements
Article 4

Principle excluding prior authorisation
1. Member States shall lay down in their legislation that access to the activity of Information Society service provider may not be made subject to prior authorisation or any other requirement the effect of which is to make such access dependent on a decision, measure or particular act by an authority.

2. Paragraph 1 shall be without prejudice to authorisation schemes which are not specifically and exclusively targeted at Information Society services, or which are covered by Directive 97/13/EC of the European Parliament and of the Council[21].

Article 5
General information to be provided

1. Member States shall lay down in their legislation that Information Society services shall render easily accessible, in a direct and permanent manner to their recipients and competent authorities, the following information:

   (a) the name of the service provider;

   (b) the address at which the service provider is established;

---

[21] OJ L 117, 7.5.1997, p. 15.

(c) the particulars of the service provider, including his electronic-mail address, which allow him to be contacted rapidly and communicated with in a direct and effective manner;

(d) where the service provider is registered in a trade register, the trade register in which the service provider is entered and his registration number in that register;

(e) where the activity is subject to an authorisation scheme, the activities covered by the authorisation granted to the service provider and the particulars of the authority providing such authorisation;

(f) as concerns the regulated professions:

—any professional body or similar institution with which the service provider is registered;
—the professional title granted in the Member State of establishment, the applicable professional rules in the Member State of establishment and the Member States in which the Information Society services are regularly provided;

(g) where the service provider undertakes an activity that is subject to VAT, the VAT number under which he is registered with his fiscal administration.

2. Member States shall lay down in their legislation that prices of Information Society services are to be indicated accurately and unequivocally.

Section 2 Commercial communications
Article 6
Information to be provided

Member States shall lay down in their legislation that commercial communication shall comply with the following conditions:

(a) the commercial communication shall be clearly identifiable as such;

(b) the natural or legal person on whose behalf the commercial communication is made shall be clearly identifiable;

(c) promotional offers, such as discounts, premiums and gifts, where authorised, shall be clearly identifiable as such, and the conditions which are to be met to qualify for them shall be easily accessible and be presented accurately and unequivocally;

(d) promotional competitions or games, where authorised, shall be clearly identifiable as such, and the conditions for participation shall be easily accessible and be presented accurately and unequivocally.

Article 7
Unsolicited commercial communication

Member States shall lay down in their legislation that unsolicited commercial communication by electronic mail must be clearly and unequivocally identifiable as such as soon as it is received by the recipient.

Article 8
Regulated professions

1. Member States shall lay down in their legislation relating to commercial communication by regulated professions that the provision of Information Society services is authorised provided that the professional rules regarding the independence, dignity and honour of the profession, professional secrecy and fairness towards clients and other members of the profession are met.

2. Member States and the Commission shall encourage professional associations and bodies to establish codes of conduct at Community level in order to determine the types of information that can be given for the purposes of providing the Information Society service in conformity with the rules referred to in paragraph 1.

3. Where necessary in order to ensure the proper functioning of the internal market, and in the light of the codes of conduct applicable at Community level, the Commission may stipulate, in accordance with the procedure laid down in Article 23, the information referred to in paragraph 2.

Section 3 Electronic contracts
Article 9
Treatment of electronic contracts

1. Member States shall ensure that their legislation allows contracts to be concluded electronically. Member States shall in particular ensure that the legal requirements applicable to the contractual process neither prevent the effective use of electronic contracts nor result in such contracts being deprived of legal effect and validity on account of their having been made electronically.

2. Member States may lay down that paragraph 1 shall not apply to the following contracts:

   (a) contracts requiring the involvement of a notary;
   (b) contracts which, in order to be valid, are required to be registered with a public authority;

(c) contracts governed by family law;

(d) contracts governed by the law of succession.

3. The list of categories of contract provided for in paragraph 2 may be amended by the Commission in accordance with the procedure laid down in Article 23.

4. Member States shall submit to the Commission a complete list of the categories of contracts covered by the derogations provided for in paragraph 2.

Article 10
Information to be provided

1. Member States shall lay down in their legislation that, except when otherwise agreed by professional persons, the manner of the formation of a contract by electronic means shall be explained by the service provider clearly and unequivocally, and prior to the conclusion of the contract. The information to be provided shall include, in particular:

   (a) the different stages to follow to conclude the contract;

   (b) whether or not the concluded contract will be filed and whether it will be accessible;

   (c) the expedients for correcting handling errors.

2. Member States shall provide in their legislation that the different steps to be followed for concluding a contract electronically shall be set out in such a way as to ensure that parties can give their full and informed consent.

3. Member States shall lay down in their legislation that, except when otherwise agreed by professional parties, the service providers shall indicate any codes of conduct to which they subscribe and information on how those codes can be consulted electronically.

Article 11
Moment at which the contract is concluded

1. Member States shall lay down in their legislation that, save where otherwise agreed by professional persons, in cases where a recipient, in accepting a service provider's offer, is required to give his consent through technological means, such as clicking on an icon, the following principles apply:

   (a) the contract is concluded when the recipient of the service:
       —has received from the service provider, electronically, an acknowledgment of receipt of the recipient's acceptance, and
       —has confirmed receipt of the acknowledgment of receipt;

(b) acknowledgment of receipt is deemed to be received and confirmation is deemed to have been given when the parties to whom they are addressed are able to access them;

(c) acknowledgment of receipt by the service provider and confirmation of the service recipient shall be sent as quickly as possible.

2. Member States shall lay down in their legislation that, save where otherwise agreed by professional persons, the service provider shall make available to the recipient of the service appropriate means allowing him to identify and correct handling errors.

Section 4 Liability of intermediaries
Article 12
Mere conduit

1. Where an Information Society service is provided that consists of the transmission in a communication network of information provided by the recipient of the service, or the provision of access to a communication network, Member States shall provide in their legislation that the provider of such a service shall not be liable, otherwise than under a prohibitory injunction, for the information transmitted, on condition that the provider:

(a) does not initiate the transmission;

(b) does not select the receiver of the transmission; and

(c) does not select or modify the information contained in the transmission.

2. The acts of transmission and of provision of access referred to in paragraph 1 include the automatic, intermediate and transient storage of the information transmitted in so far as this takes place for the sole purpose of carrying out the transmission in the communication network, and provided that the information is not stored for any period longer than is reasonably necessary for the transmission.

Article 13
Caching

Where an Information Society service is provided that consists in the transmission in a communication network of information provided by a recipient of the service, Member States shall provide in their legislation that the provider shall not be liable, otherwise than under a prohibitory injunction, for the automatic, intermediate and temporary storage of that information, performed for the sole purpose of making more efficient the information's onward transmission to other recipients of the service upon their request, on condition that:

(a) the provider does not modify the information;
(b) the provider complies with conditions on access to the information;
(c) the provider complies with rules regarding the updating of the information, specified in a manner consistent with industrial standards;
(d) the provider does not interfere with the technology, consistent with industrial standards, used to obtain data on the use of the information; and
(e) the provider acts expeditiously to remove or to bar access to the information upon obtaining actual knowledge of one of the following:

—the information at the initial source of the transmission has been removed from the network;
—access to it has been barred;
—a competent authority has ordered such removal or barring.

Article 14
Hosting

1. Where an Information Society service is provided that consists in the storage of information provided by a recipient of the service, Member States shall provide in their legislation that the provider shall not be liable, otherwise than under a prohibitory injunction, for the information stored at the request of a recipient of the service, on condition that:

   (a) the provider does not have actual knowledge that the activity is illegal and, as regards claims for damages, is not aware of facts or circumstances from which illegal activity is apparent; or
   (b) the provider, upon obtaining such knowledge or awareness, acts expeditiously to remove or to disable access to the information.

2. Paragraph 1 shall not apply when the recipient of the service is acting under the authority or the control of the provider.

Article 15
No obligation to monitor

1. Member States shall not impose a general obligation on providers, when providing the services covered by Articles 12 and 14, to monitor the information which they transmit or store, nor a general obligation actively to seek facts or circumstances indicating illegal activity.

2. Paragraph 1 shall not affect any targeted, temporary surveillance activities required by national judicial authorities in accordance with national legislation to safeguard national security, defence, public security and for the prevention, investigation, detection and prosecution of criminal offences.

CHAPTER III
IMPLEMENTATION
Article 16
Codes of conduct

1. Member States and the Commission shall encourage:

    (a) the drawing-up of codes of conduct at Community level, by trade and professional associations or organisations designed to contribute to the proper implementation of Articles 5 to 15;
    (b) the transmission of draft codes of conduct at national or Community level to the Commission so that the latter may examine their compatibility with Community law;
    (c) the accessibility of these codes of conduct in the Community languages by electronic means;
    (d) the communication to the Member States and the Commission, by professional associations or organisations, of their assessment of the application of their codes of conduct and their impact upon practices, habits or customs relating to electronic commerce.

2. In so far as they may be concerned, consumer associations shall be involved in the drafting and implementation of codes of conduct drawn up according to point (a) of paragraph 1.

Article 17
Out-of-court dispute settlement

1. Member States shall ensure that, in the event of disagreement between an Information Society service provider and its recipient, their legislation allows the effective use of out-of-court schemes fsor dispute settlement, including appropriate electronic means.

2. Member States shall ensure that bodies responsible for the out-of-court settlement of consumer disputes apply, whilst abiding by Community law, the principles of independence and transparency, of adversarial techniques, procedural efficacy, legality of the decision, and freedom of the parties and of representation.

3. Member States shall encourage bodies responsible for out-of-court dispute settlement to inform the Commission of the decisions they take regarding Information Society services and to transmit any other information on the practices, usages or customs relating to electronic commerce.

Article 18
Court actions

1. Member States shall ensure that effective court actions can be brought against Information Society services' activities, by allowing the rapid adoption of interim measures designed to remedy any alleged infringement and to prevent any further impairment of the interests involved.

2. Acts in breach of the national provisions incorporating Articles 5 to 15 of this Directive which affect consumers' interests shall constitute infringements within the meaning of Article 1(2) of Directive 98/27/EC of the European Parliament and Council[22].

Article 19
Cooperation between authorities

1. Member States shall ensure that their competent authorities have the appropriate powers of supervision and investigation necessary to implement this Directive effectively and that service providers supply those authorities with the requisite information.

2. Member States shall ensure that their national authorities cooperate with the authorities of other Member States; they shall, to that end, appoint a contact person, whose coordinates they shall communicate to the other Member States and to the Commission.

3. Member States shall, as quickly as possible, provide the assistance and information requested by authorities of other Member States or by the Commission, including by appropriate electronic means.

4. Member States shall establish, within their administration, contact points which shall be accessible electronically and from which recipients and service providers may:

   (a) obtain information on their contractual rights and obligations;
   (b) obtain the particulars of authorities, associations or organisations from which recipients of services may obtain information about their rights or with whom they may file complaints; and
   (c) receive assistance in the event of disputes.

5. Member States shall ensure that their competent authorities inform the Commission of any administrative or judicial decisions taken in their territory regarding disputes relating to Information Society services and practices, usages and customs relating to electronic commerce.

---

[22] OJ L 166, 11.6.1998, p. 51.

6. The rules governing cooperation between national authorities as referred to in paragraphs 2 to 5 shall be laid down by the Commission in accordance with the procedure set out in Article 23.

7. Member States may ask the Commission to convene urgently the committee referred to in Article 23 in order to examine difficulties over the application of Article 3(1).

Article 20
Electronic media

The Commission may take measures, in accordance with the procedure provided for in Article 23, to ensure the proper functioning of electronic media between Member States, as referred to in Articles 17(1) and 19(3) and (4).

Article 21
Sanctions

Member States shall determine the sanctions applicable to infringements of national provisions adopted pursuant to this Directive and shall take all measures necessary to ensure that they are enforced. The sanctions they provide for shall be effective, proportionate and dissuasive. Member States shall notify these measures to the Commission no later than the date specified in Article 25 and shall inform it of all subsequent amendments to those measures without delay.

CHAPTER IV
EXCLUSIONS FROM SCOPE AND DEROGATIONS
Article 22
Exclusions and derogations

1. This Directive shall not apply to:
    (a) taxation;
    (b) the field covered by Directive 95/46/EC of the European Parliament and of the Council[23];
    (c) the activities of Information Society services referred to in Annex I. This list of activities may be amended by the Commission in accordance with the procedure laid down by Article 23.
2. Article 3 shall not apply to the fields referred to in Annex II.

---

[23] OJ L 281, 23.11.1995, p. 31.

3. By way of derogation from Article 3(2), and without prejudice to court action, the competent authorities of Member States may take such measures restricting the freedom to provide an Information Society service as are consistent with Community law and with the following provisions:

(a) the measures shall be:
    (i) necessary for one of the following reasons:
        —public policy, in particular the protection of minors, or the fight against any incitement to hatred on grounds of race, sex, religion or nationality,
        —the protection of public health,
        —public security,
        —consumer protection;
    (ii) taken against an Information Society service which prejudices the objectives referred to in point (i) or which presents a serious and grave risk of prejudice to those objectives,
    (iii) proportionate to those objectives;
(b) prior to taking the measures in question, the Member State has:
    —asked the Member State referred to in Article 3(1) to take measures and the latter did not take such measures, or the latter were inadequate;
    —notified the Commission and the Member State in which the service provider is established of its intention to take such measures;
(c) Member States may lay down in their legislation that, in the case of urgency, the conditions stipulated in point (b) do not apply. Where this is the case, the measures shall be notified in the shortest possible time to the Commission and to the Member State in which the service provider is established, indicating the reasons for which the Member State considers that there is urgency.
(d) the Commission may decide on the compatibility of the measures with Community law. Where it adopts a negative decision, the Member States shall refrain from taking any proposed measures or shall be required to urgently put an end to the measures in question.

CHAPTER V
ADVISORY COMMITTEE AND FINAL PROVISIONS
Article 23
Committee

The Commission shall be assisted by a committee of an advisory nature composed of the representatives of the Member States and chaired by the representative of the Commission.

The representative of the Commission shall submit to the committee a draft of the measures to be taken. The committee shall deliver its opinion on the draft, within a time-limit which the chairman may lay down according to the urgency of the matter, if necessary by taking a vote.

The opinion shall be recorded in the minutes; in addition, each Member State shall have the right to ask to have its position recorded in the minutes.

The Commission shall take the utmost account of the opinion delivered by the committee. It shall inform the committee of the manner in which its opinion has been taken into account.

Article 24
Re-examination

Not later than three years after the adoption of this Directive, and thereafter every two years, the Commission shall submit to the European Parliament, the Council and the Economic and Social Committee a report on the application of this Directive, accompanied, where necessary, by proposals for adapting it to developments in the field of Information Society services.

Article 25
Implementation

Member States shall bring into force the laws, regulations and administrative provisions necessary to comply with this Directive within one year of its entry into force. They shall forthwith inform the Commission thereof.

When Member States adopt these provisions, these shall contain a reference to this Directive or shall be accompanied by such reference at the time of their official publication. The methods of making such reference shall be laid down by Member States.

Article 26
Entry into force

This Directive shall enter into force on the twentieth day following that of its publication in the *Official Journal of the European Communities*.

Article 27
Addressees

This Directive is addressed to the Member States.

Done at Brussels,

For the European Parliament   *For the Council*
The President   *The President*

ANNEX I
Activities excluded from the scope of application of the Directive

Information Society services' activities, as referred to in Article 22(1), which are not covered by this Directive:

—the activities of notaries;
—the representation of a client and defence of his interests before the courts;
—gambling activities, excluding those carried out for commercial communication purposes.

ANNEX II
Derogations from Article 3

As referred to in Article 22(2) in which Article 3 does not apply:

—copyright, neighbouring rights, rights referred to in Directive 87/54/EEC[24] and Directive 96/9/EC[25] as well as industrial property rights;
—the emission of electronic money by institutions in respect of which Member States have applied one of the derogations provided for in Article 7(1) of Directive . . ./. . ./EC[26];
—Article 44 paragraph 2 of Directive 85/611/EEC[27];
—Article 30 and Title IV of Directive 92/49/EEC[28], Title IV of

[24] Council Directive 87/54/EEC of 16 December 1986 on the legal protection of topographies of semiconductor products; OJ L 24, 27.1.1987, p. 36.

[25] Directive 96/9/EC of the European Parliament and of the Council of 11 March 1996 on the legal protection of databases; OJ L 77, 27.3.1996, p. 20.

[26] European Parliament and Council Directive . . ./. . ./EC of . . . [on the taking up and the prudential supervision of the business of electronic money instituions].

[27] Council Directive 85/611/EEC of 20 December 1985 on the coordination of laws, regulations and administrative provisions relating to undertaking for collective investment in transferable securities (UCITS), OJ L 375, 31.12.1985, p. 3, as last amended by Directive 95/26/EC of the European Parliament and of the Council (OJ L 168, 18.7.1995, p. 7).

[28] Council Directive 92/49/EEC of 18 June 1992 on the coordination of laws, regulations and administrative provisions relating to direct insurance other than life assurance and amending Directives 73/239/EEC and 88/357/EEC (third non-life insurance Directive) OJ L 228, 11.8.1992, p. 1, as amended by Directive 95/26/EC.

Directive 92/96/EEC[29], Articles 7 and 8 of Directive 88/357/EEC[30] and Article 4 of Directive 90/619/EEC[31];
—contractual obligations concerning consumer contracts;
—unsolicited commercial communications by electronic mail, or by an equivalent individual communication.

[29] Council Directive 92/56/EEC of 10 November 1992 on the coordination of laws, regulations and administrative provisions relating to direct life insurance and amending Directives 79/267/EEC and 90/619/EEC (third life assurance Directive), OJ L 360, 9.12.1992, p. 1, as amended by Directive 95/26/EC.

[30] Second Council Directive 88/357/EEC of 22 June 1988 on the coordination of laws, regulations and administrative provisions relating to direct insurance other than life assurance and laying down provisions to facilitate the effective exercise of freedom to provide services and amending Directive 73/239/EEC, OJ L 172, 4.7.1988, p. 1, as last amended by Directive 92/49/EC.

[31] Council Directive of 8 November 1990 on the coordination of laws, regulations and administrative provisions relating to direct life assurance laying down provisions to facilitate the effective exercise of freedom to provide services and amending Directive 79/267/EEC, OJ L 330, 29.11.1990, p. 50, as amended by Directive 92/96/EEC.

Useful Web Addresses

Within Europe

EU homepage, containing links to all the institutions, Commission Directorate-Generals XV (internal market) and XXIV (consumer protection) being particularly relevant to electronic commerce.

http://www.europa.eu.int

Information Society Project Office, a unit within the European Commission which is the Union's principal electronic commerce Web portal. Contains information and links on research, studies, discussion lists, and technical, business and regulatory issues.

http://www.ispo.cec.be

European Parliament, including a Legislative Observatory through which the passage of draft legislation can be tracked.

http://www.europarl.eu.int

International Organisations

International Chamber of Commerce —GUIDEC—General Usage for International Digitally Ensured Commerce

http://www.iccwbo.org/ guidec2.htm

United Nations Commission on International Trade Law, includes Model Law on Electronic Commerce with Guide to Enactment

http://www.un.or.at/uncitral/

Organisation for Economic Cooperation and Development E-commerce page

http://www.oecd.org/dsti/sti/it/ec

World Trade Organisation

http://www.wto.org

World Intellectual Property Organisation

http://www.wipo.org

Other

The National Conference of Commissioners on Uniform State Laws (site contains the US Uniform Electronic Transactions Act, under the heading Uniform Electronic Communication in Contractual Transactions Act).	http://www.law.upenn.edu/ library/ulc/ulc.htm
McBride Baker and Cole—Summary of World-wide Electronic Commerce and Digital Signature Legislation with links.	http://www.mbc.com/ds_sum.html
American Bar Association Electronic Commerce Pages	http://www.abanet.org/scitech/ec/
The US President's Information Infrastructure Task Force	http://www.iitf.nist.gov/
US Government Electronic Commerce Policy	http://www.ecommerce.gov/
Utah Digital Signature Act 1996	http://www.commerce.state.ut.us/ web/commerce/digsig/act.htm
Australian Attorney General's Electronic Commerce Expert Group Report	http://law.gov.au/aghome/ advisory/eceg/eceg.htm
Internet Law and Policy Forum, a neutral forum for the discussion of Internet -related issues.	http://www.ilpf.org
US-EU Transatlantic Consumer Dialogue recommendations on electronic commerce.	http://www.tacd.org/meeting1/ electronic.html

Index